Stronger than Espresso®
Participant Guide
2nd Edition

Deanne,

Thank you for all you do for the Lord's Kingdom! Blessings with every step.

Your sister in christ.

Brooke

Stronger than Espresso®
Participant Guide
2nd Edition

Jolt Awake!
Your Guide to Victory Over Domestic Violence and
Patterns of Abuse.

by Brooke Jones

United States of America

For information contact Stronger than Espresso, Inc. at www.strongerthanespresso.com. Stronger than Espresso® books can be purchased in bulk for church, business, educational or sales promotional use. Please send an inquiry to info@strongerthanespresso.com.

Cover designed by Teresa Bohn.

This book is dedicated to –

Rick, Austin & Ivy

The moments God kissed my forehead

And

To my beloved husband
A man of God and a man who believed in me even when I did not.
Thank you for your encouragement, love and spiritual covering.

Table of Contents

Illustrations

Foreword

Stronger than Espresso® is a comprehensive guide for victims of domestic violence and abuse. The author has provided a step-by-step guide of activities that meets the learner at her own level. Whether the woman is just beginning her journey to freedom or a seasoned learner, each participant will find relevant activities that bring clarity to the recovery process from domestic abuse.

Brooke Jones has birthed an action plan for recovery and redemption for victims of abuse. She has carefully woven the need for a spiritual Christ-based attitude with effective exercises and activities to help the participant emerge from a defeated self-image to a vibrant worthy person. The organization of the book is structured to move from the simple to complex along with exercises that are both fundamental and challenging. This book provides a tool to recovery for any victim of abuse. Sit back, grab a cup of coffee, and become *Stronger than Espresso*.

Paula Witt, Ed. D.

Brooke Jones has been blessed with an inner strength that provides her with thoughtful insight, humility and reassuring wisdom. Brooke and I first connected in 1995. Since then she has used her life experiences to reach out to others thereby growing and transforming her own life.

Stronger than Espresso® is a guide to help you learn, change and grow. Through the Stronger than Espresso journey you will be guided through points of self-discovery. This takes place by being honest with yourself and your situation. You then relearn old patterns and grow into the person you were meant to be.

Stronger than Espresso® is exactly what I could have used years ago and I know it will be a rewarding experience for you.

Gail Clark, Author
Heart Praises

Continued on next page

She sat alone, hurting and afraid, bruised physically and emotionally from the outburst that just ended. If she made a move to free herself and her children from another outburst of anger and even physical or sexual violence... she would lose the foundations of security that were all she knew. A place to stay dry and food to eat. She would have to get a first or second job and raise the kids while running for her life. The choice was too great and undoubting. And her sense of self-worth had diminished to nothing...

Perhaps you find yourself or someone you know in a situation similar to this statement. If so, then you have arrived at the right place. *Stronger than Espresso®* is a manual of Hope, lighting a path to guide women living in fear to safety, and instilling an understanding of the true value that God places in you.

Stronger Than Espresso is your opportunity to break free from the chains of violence. In this book, Brooke provides a step-by-step process that will enable the reader and group leaders to chart a course to freedom from the bondage of domestic or sexual violence. It is supported with group dynamics to enable you to know you are not alone, because taking this next step of your journey is easier when someone is beside you and the path is lit. The foundational principles of each step of Stronger Than Espresso are weighted in God's word. As a minister of Celebrate Recovery®, I have found where in even the most difficult and darkest of circumstances, God's word brings light, hope and power to the issue. As you work through each lesson in this book, you will find key scriptures to memorize and use in time of need. You will be nourished with encouragement, hope and instruction to be able to believe in yourself again and to be the person God created in you.... Because you are "fearfully and wonderfully made" Ps 139:14 (NIV). Brooke has lived where you live. And she has spent thousands of hours preparing for you in prayer, study, and in tears. I know, because I have watched her. Welcome to your new life.

Rick Jones
CEO, Soulful Creations, LLC
Celebrate Recovery® Ministry Leader
Husband

Preface

Stronger than Espresso® specializes in a Christian approach to connect, encourage, educate, coach, mentor, and train survivors of domestic abuse. It offers a place of HOPE where women can HEAL and HELP others claim victory over adversity.

The *Stronger than Espresso®* program began as a "God whisper" and specializes in encouragement, education, coaching and mentoring services. This training program focuses on supporting victims of domestic violence when they are finally ready to let go of their past and help them claim victory after adversity. The training program is built with variations in mind to meet your needs. The Participant Guide is for individual use alone, or to achieve the full benefit of the program, join classes in your area or online. Using the Leader Guide, you can conduct classes in your church, in your community or in your home after attending a training session. Mentorship connections are created for a support system during the coursework and beyond.

As a survivor of domestic abuse I know the journey to recovery is long and difficult. In the critical stages of my abuse, there were resources for emergency care and access to counseling that was desperately needed. The real challenge for me was in the years to follow. Low self-esteem, self-doubt, fear, anxiety, and depression remained. Unhealthy habits, self-destructive behaviors, symptoms of post-traumatic stress disorder, inability to concentrate, and panic attacks were overwhelming. Challenged with the prospect of identifying a healthy love or establishing a new relationship was daunting. In this journey, God's love was always there but I never gave it the attention or trust that it deserved. It wasn't until I finally accepted His love into my life that the lasting journey to recovery could begin.

As a woman I learned that I could be free from my own repeat patterns, bad relationships and unhealthy coping mechanisms. Trusting God was the key ingredient I had missed. Once I learned to trust God I finally restored to a healthy, vibrant individual.

As a mother I knew that I had to be the best "me" I could for my kids.

As an educator I believe that individuals learn and retain information best when they connect with others. The educational process is more vibrant, creative and long-lasting when groups interact versus being alone. Rebuilding takes time and hard work, and you need to connect with others to help along the way.

You are Stronger than Espresso! Visit our website to connect www.strongerthanespresso.com. Together let's end domestic violence; one person at a time.

Cheering you on! Brooke Jones

Acknowledgements

To everyone who willingly shared ideas and input for this book I offer my heartfelt thanks. Praise to God for His "God whispers" and who really made all this possible.

I want to thank my husband for his love, encouragement and unending belief in my dream. Even when I doubted along the way, he knew the perfect words to strengthen my confidence. His positive words, creativity and time as my sounding board during the program's development is a blessing.

My trusted advisors and friends: Dr. Paula Witt, Gail Clark and Karen Jordan for their opinions, tireless hours reading and proofing drafts. Their encouragement kept me focused on taking the next right step during the program development. I would like to thank the Domestic Violence workers that were available during my emergency needs and difficult times. Thanks to the talented and dedicated staff of the National Network to End Domestic Violence (NNEDV), Hope's Door, and Genesis Women's Shelter in Texas for their time and input along the way. Thanks to all the domestic violence programs around the world for their tireless efforts to bring an end to domestic violence. Thanks to the professors at Ashford University who provided encouragement along the way as I developed portions of this program to meet course assignments earning my Master's degree. Thanks to my friends at First National Bank Texas for always being supportive of my desires to develop training curriculum to serve my ministry calling.

I want to applaud Teresa Bohn for her cover art design and development. Thank you to Jens Bröcher for the web design and his help to understand the "tech-talk" to move my dream forward. I would like to thank the pastoral staff at Genesis Church, McKinney, Texas for their support and spiritual covering of prayer during the curriculum development. Blessed be my friends and family who prayed as these seeds were sown to advance God's kingdom.

Thanks for buying this book and having the courage to redefine your life. Greetings to new Stronger than Espresso participants and leaders forming local programs or joining online around the globe. Welcome to the Stronger than Espresso family.

You are Stronger than Espresso!   It is time to jolt awake and claim victory over adversity!

Stronger than Espresso®
Participant Guide
2nd Edition

Jolt Awake!
Your Guide to Victory Over Domestic Violence and
Patterns of Abuse.

By Brooke Jones

Welcome

Overview

Introduction   Thank you for being here today. God has called you for a purpose. Stronger than Espresso is the first step to fulfill God's purpose in your life. Find Victory over the impact domestic violence and patterns of abuse have had on your life. Time to Jolt Awake and become Stronger than Espresso.

Vision   Connecting survivors of domestic violence around the globe to restore, encourage and educate on how to finally break free of the past and understand the power in God's love to heal and bring hope.

Mission   Stronger than Espresso specializes in a Christian approach to connect, encourage, educate, coach, mentor, and train survivors of domestic abuse. Offering a place of HOPE where women can HEAL and HELP others claim victory over adversity.

Purpose   Stronger than Espresso is a Christ-based program exclusively designed for women survivors of domestic abuse, who are ready to jolt awake and transform their lives. Even after surviving the crisis and trauma of abuse, many women still struggle with low self-esteem, confusing emotions and other negative patterns. Provide resources for victims of domestic violence:

- Encourage.
- Educate — self learning in a safe environment, group learning.
- Reveal God's love — it is okay to be loved as we are.
- Deliver hope and restoration.
- Establish healthy beliefs in ourselves.
- Create healthy boundaries for our future.
- Connect women together through course work, mentorships and coaches.

Continued on next page

Overview, Continued

Commitment

Stronger than Espresso's commitment:

- Everyone deserves a life without abuse.

- You are Stronger than Espresso and can escape the cycle of domestic abuse and be free from the residual impact patterns of abuse has had on your life.

- Hope, grace and love are waiting for you.

- With God all things are possible!

- God's timing is perfect and now is your time to transform.

Guiding Principles

Restoration = Love, Understanding, Knowledge, Wisdom

Foundational Scripture

"This is the message we have heard from him and declare to you: God is light; in him there is no darkness at all. If we claim to have fellowship with him yet walk in the darkness we lie and do not live by the truth. But if we walk in the light, as he is in the light, we have fellowship with one another, and the blood of Jesus, his Son, purifies us from all sin."

1 John 1:5–7 (NIV)

Value

Stronger than Espresso® classes add value to your church or community by offering a low-cost, community solution to connect women who need encouragement, hope and emotional support to understand the pattern of domestic violence. Transforming lives. Connecting women. Building leaders. Breaking the cycle.

Continued on next page

Overview, Continued

Ultimate power God is in the house!

Stronger than Espresso has God and His power at the center.

Through Him *"All things are possible."* **—Matthew 19:26**

"We are not given a spirit of fear, but of power, love and a sound mind." **—2 Timothy 1:7**

What to expect **What can women expect from a Stronger than Espresso class?**

- A safe place to learn and fellowship with other women.
- Dynamic and interactive classes to enhance learning.
- Reflect on past, analysis of present and create vision for future.
- Use of the Stronger than Espresso® guidebooks.
- Access to online class content.

Stages of healing There are five stages for the Stronger than Espresso healing process:

1. A Jolt Awake moment to come out of denial to receive help.
2. Identify coping skills used to survive.
3. Understanding abusive relationships.
4. Building your self-esteem.
5. Redefining your life in terms of your 7 Key Ingredients: God, Body, Soul, Mind, Words, Lessons and Relationships

Overview, Continued

Online Support

Each of the Classes has supplemental resources for each lesson:

- Downloadable videos, podcasts, images, documents are accessible free for all STE class participants.
  www.strongerthanespresso.com/classsupplements

  Password: **miracles**

- Free downloadable self-help brochures

- STE Sisterhood

- Accountability

Thank you

Thank for you for listening to God's call.

Introduction

You can be free   This workbook is a woman's guide to claim victory over adversity over domestic abuse and other patterns of abuse in your life. You may be a survivor of domestic abuse by an intimate partner, sexual abuse, emotional or verbal abuse. You may be a survivor of abusive patterns from your family of origin and these memories and events follow you from childhood. These patterns of abuse keep resurfacing in your life and you are ready, oh so ready, to be free!

You may still be in your abusive situation, or perhaps you recently left. Many of you left the abuse months, even years ago, but are still affected by the hurt you suffered in an abusive relationship.

You feel trapped by your inability to grow beyond the hurt and to fully restore your life. The fear and control remains and continues to bind you long after the situation has changed. Regardless of where you are; you CAN be healed and finally free.

All are welcome   Domestic violence happens in every race, religion, culture, economic and gender group:

- One out of every three women will be abused at some point in her life.
- Battery is the single major cause of injury to women.
- A woman is more likely to be killed by a male partner (or former partner) than any other person.
- About 4,000 women die each year due to domestic violence.
- Of the total domestic violence homicides, about 75% of the victims were killed as they attempted to leave the relationship or after the relationship had ended.
- On average, a woman will leave an abusive relationship seven times before she leaves for good.

If you are currently being abused or have survived abuse, you are not alone.

Continued on next page

Introduction

Class Expectations

What are your expectations for this course:

-
-
-
-

My story in a nutshell

At the first class you will be asked to share a little about you. Jot notes here to provide a five minute description of your story.

"Survivors of domestic violence and patterns of abuse live all around us, and they fail to recognize how beautiful they are. We need to get the word out... We must help women know they are worthy of being loved."

Brooke Jones, Author, Stronger than Espresso

Continued on next page

Introduction, Continued

Evaluate

Are you still in an abusive relationship?

- Do you "stuff" your pain deep inside?

- Are you frustrated because you have tried everything, but still the abuse won't stop?

- Have you told lies to your family and friends about the relationship?

- Are you emotionally struggling and feel you have no place to turn?

- Have you become a hollow shell of what used to be a vibrant, loving person?

- Are you angry because people just don't understand why you stay in this relationship?

- Do you feel you can no longer continue to exist this way?

- Do you know he/she is wrong for you but you can't stop calling, texting or making contact with him/her?

Are you out of the relationship, but still held captive by your past?

- Has your emptiness and loneliness eroded your life?

- Are you confused about why you keep repeating the same bad relationships?

- Have you been gone from the relationship for a while, but still can't get "over it"?

- Do you struggle believing you are worthy of a new life?

- Is it hard to imagine that you were made as a perfect creation by God?

If you have answered *Yes* to any of these questions, the Stronger than Espresso® program is for you! Get ready to jolt awake. Rebuild your life.

Continued on next page

Introduction, Continued

Who will benefit from this book?

Women who:

- Have left their abusive relationship(s) but still cannot reach their full potential. You are still holding on to low self-esteem and other hurtful behaviors due to the abuse you survived. Even still, you have hope that your life can be transformed.

- Are still in an abusive relationship, but are ready to emerge, this book can help you, but you still need emergency/critical care at this time.

If you are in danger contact a local family justice center, women's shelter or dial 9-1-1 to assist you. You can also contact the National Domestic Violence hotline at 1-800-799-7233 to help you find resources in your area. As you begin to change patterns and break away your risks can increase significantly!

"Then you will call, and the Lord will answer; you will cry for help, and he will say: Here am I."

— Isaiah 58:9 (New International Version)

How to use this book?

Each Chapter includes activities designed to teach and discover your thoughts and feelings. Distinguishing the many facets of abuse and understanding your role in the cycle can lead to healing. By the conclusion of this program, you will be armed with answers and insights to build a new foundation. Creating your action plan will begin your freedom from your past.

God's healing power is amazing. Self-dedication and commitment will be required to complete this transformation. This workbook can be used independently by an individual, by a leader who conducts small groups, or online where available. For online groups see www.strongerthanespresso.com for more details.

"Jesus looked at them and said, 'With man this is impossible, but with God all things are possible.'"

— Matthew 19:26 (NIV)

Continued on next page

Introduction, Continued

How to use this book?
(continued)

Take time to work the exercises, answer the questions and analyze your feelings. Be honest with yourself. This is one time when you don't have to pretend or hold a hollow smile for anyone. The more honest you are with your feelings the better equipped you are to rebuild a new foundation and a new way of life. If you have a question about an activity or need help with the workbook, visit www.strongerthanespresso.com for assistance.

"14 Build up, build up, prepare the road! Remove the obstacles out of the way of my people…18 I have seen his ways, but I will heal him; I will guide him and restore comfort to him, 19 creating praise on the lips of the mourners in Israel. Peace, peace, to those far and near, says the Lord. 'And I will heal them.'"
— **Isaiah 57:14, 18, 19 (NIV)**

The guarantee:

- God removes obstacles

- He will heal and guide you, regardless of any mistakes you have made

- You can have peace and be restored

What to expect

This workbook guides you on a personal journey to discover your patterns of behavior, to identify abusive relationships, to restore self-esteem and to build a plan of action to redefine your life. What makes this book different is that it is based on God's word. It allows God's love to emerge during the healing process to make your transformation last for a lifetime.

Icons are used throughout the book to help organize the information:

Icon	Purpose
	Learning Activity
	Testimonial Quote
	Scripture Reference

Continued on next page

Introduction, Continued

Why I wrote this book?

This book is about hope.

Has God ever whispered in your ear? Creating this program was a whisper from God many years ago, after I had survived domestic abuse. He told me that I had to share what I had learned in my journey. It happened when I accepted His great love into my heart where sustainable healing occurred.

Over the years, I endured numerous abusive relationships and pulled myself out of the valley many times. Bad relationships and bad choices. My life was a repeat pattern of disappointment. Identifying these patterns through His love helped me heal lifelong hurts stemming back to childhood. Once our lives are enriched by His grace and love, true healing and transformation occur! Without His love, the recovery process is only temporary.

During my rebuilding process I was exposed to a combination of therapy programs, women's crisis centers, various educational and court-sponsored Victim Assistance programs. When you combine information, connect with other survivors and allow the healing power of God's love into your life – A miracle happens!

Infused with God's love our lives change. God is the one of miracles, forgiveness and grace. This workbook was created to provide a Biblical approach to the road to recovery for anyone experiencing domestic abuse.

"Once He changes you, you are never, ever the same."

Brooke Jones

Your great work

"[8]For it is by grace you have been saved, through faith – and this not from yourselves, it is the gift of God – [9]not by works, so that no one can boast. [10]For we are God's workmanship, created in Christ Jesus to do good works, which God prepared in advance for us to do." **— Ephesians 2:8-10 (NIV)**

Remember:

- Grace is God's gift to you; it does not need to be earned

- God made you, and He does great work, so You = Great work

- You were created for a purpose

Continued on next page

Introduction, Continued

Objectives of this book

The Stronger than Espresso® program can be used several ways:

1. Individuals can study the Participant Guide independently.
2. Women can join a STE class in the area.
3. Women can train to be a leader and launch STE classes in a new area. Leader guide and training is available.

The Lessons will contribute to the following learning objectives:

Figure 1. Stronger than Espresso® Learning Objectives. Source: Stronger than Espresso, Inc. © 2014.

At Stronger than Espresso® we believe that Jesus Christ is our Savior and the way to eternal life. Our programs are based on these objectives and founded on this scripture:

"[5] This is the message we have heard from him and declare to you: God is light; in him there is no darkness at all. [6] If we claim to have fellowship with him yet walk in the darkness, we lie and do not live by truth. [7] But if we walk in the light, as he is in the light, we have fellowship with one another, and the blood of Jesus, his Son, purifies us from all sin."

— 1 John 1: 5-7 (NIV)

Continued on next page

Introduction, Continued

Personal commitment

As a survivor of domestic abuse I can say that I was finally jolted awake and able to recognize my abusive situation. The sad part was I was just repeating the same abusive relationships again and again. Even though I finally escaped, it still took another decade to learn and accept how much God loves me.

Finally, I can claim victory over my adversity. I no longer have to be in a broken life-long cycle.

The key ingredient to this program is God's love and the ability to heal with other women. Connect, encourage and grow when you dive into the program and build friends in the Stronger than Espresso® Sisterhood.

I have now become Stronger than Espresso, and so can you. Get ready and drink up. You are Stronger than Espresso® and can claim victory over adversity!

Brooke Jones, Author& Founder, Stronger than Espresso®

Scripture summary

A list of scriptures will be noted at the end of each Chapter. Reference to the learning objective they support will be identified. Use these scriptures for personal study, reflection and prayer time. Ask God to reveal to you areas that need prayer and healing.

Scripture	Objective	Personal Thoughts
Isaiah 58:9	Self-esteem — Confidence	
Matthew 19:26	Self-esteem — Confidence	
Isaiah 57:14, 18, 19	Spirituality — Love	
Ephesians 2:8–10	Spirituality — Love	
1 John 1:5–7	Connections — Coach	

Jolt Awake!
Your Guide to Victory Over Domestic Violence

Sections Summary

Introduction

Drop your mask! Release your shackles!

There is hope. The way you feel right now can change. Let God infuse you with his love and light. Jolt awake and escape domestic abuse, forever.

Begin to live the way God designed your life and finally, be free.

Contents

This publication contains the following Sections:

Topic	See Page
Section 1: The Awakening: You Are Not Alone	17
Section 2: Recognizing Patterns of Behavior	53
Section 3: Understanding Abusive Relationships	153
Section 4: Build Your Self-Esteem	213
Section 5: Redefine Your Life	249

Course Objectives

Upon completion of this course, participants will be able to:

- Define how God's love can transform your life.
- Identify the characteristics of abusive relationships.
- Recognize reoccurring coping patterns of behavior and develop alternative responses.
- Reestablish new inner music and self-talk.
- Describe medical impact surviving an abusive relationship.
- Demonstrate the ability to rebuild self-esteem.
- Build a personal relationship with God to gain knowledge, wisdom and understanding.
- Create a new life-action plan using the seven measures of perfection.

Section 1: The Awakening: You Are Not Alone

Overview

Introduction

You are not alone. One out of three women has been abused. You may have escaped the abuse but the hurt, pain and memories can still bind you. This limits you from becoming all that God's designed for your life. Hope, love and freedom await you.

"...You have come to your royal position for such a time as this."

— **Esther 4:14**

Contents

This section contains the following topics:

Topic	See Page
Chapter 1: Espresso and You	19
Chapter 2: Your "Aha" Moment	29
Chapter 3: Feelings Assessment	35
Chapter 4: Coping Mechanisms	41
Section One Summary	51

Objectives

When completing this Section, you will be able to:

- Identify current feelings and create solutions to change.
- Describe the moment when abuse could no longer continue.
- Recognize that you are not alone.
- Identify personal patterns of coping behavior and reestablish new methods.
- Describe God's love for you and the blessings He has put in your life.

Notes:

Chapter 1: Espresso and You

Purpose

The purpose of Chapter 1 is to introduce you to the Stronger than Espresso program, begin to build relationships with your classmates, and spark your self-awareness process to discover areas of opportunities and growth.

Definition: Espresso

Espresso is a complex beverage with three vital parts the heart, body, and crema.[1] The crema' is the reddish brown foam that floats on the top and is the distinguishing part of an authentic espresso. It is what gives each cup life and uniqueness. You are like a complex cup of espresso with a heart, body and your spirit is the crema that gives life and uniqueness.

> "The key to espresso is to realize that it always has further potential. By changing any one factor you can improve or diminish its potential. Espresso preparation is an art that demands the precision and dedication of science. I have never achieved, nor have ever seen a perfect espresso. A perfect espresso is more of a concept than an actuality. The beauty is that espresso is volatile and difficult. If it were easy we would develop a machine that can brew perfect espresso every time. There are so many factors involved in espresso preparation that only a human mind and passionate heart can begin to understand and control its complexity."

> Source: www.CoffeeResearch.org. *Espresso, Making a Perfect Espresso*. Copyright ©2007. Reprinted with permission of www.CoffeeResearch.org.

Continued on next page

Chapter 1: Espresso and You, Continued

Crafting a better you

What an eloquent and fabulous description of the art of crafting the perfect espresso. It teaches us that it is a skill perfected over years of practice, and is not to be taken lightly.

If you consider the life cycle of a coffee bean. It is picked off the tree. Then roasted, as if set through the fire. Next it is put through one or multiple processes. Crushed and ground are the processes it endures and the challenges the bean faces to bring it to a state of perfection. Once it is ready...it can be brewed to perfection.

You are much more valuable than a cup of coffee, but this analogy shows us that even in a simple cup of coffee there are many factors in play to craft perfection. You are a complex being and there are many factors that must be taken into consideration. Similarly, the art to crafting a better you must be perfected through similar commitment, dedication, hard work and practice.

Define a new you

Objective: Discover personal areas of opportunity and growth and begin to build relationships with others.

Continued on next page

Chapter 1: Espresso and You, Continued

Espresso Definition	Your Definition
"The key to espresso is to realize that it always has further potential.	Describe areas where you have further potential?
"By changing any one factor you can improve or diminish its potential."	What would you change to improve your potential?
"Espresso preparation is an art that demands the precision and dedication of science."	Identify areas in your life where you demonstrate precision and dedication. Identify areas where you would like to demonstrate these qualities but do not at this time.
"I have never achieved, nor have ever seen a perfect espresso."	What is the risk if you expect perfection of yourself?
"The beauty is that espresso is volatile and difficult."	Describe areas in your life where you are volatile and difficult?
"If it were easy we would develop a machine that can brew perfect espresso every time."	What is the consequence if you try the quick and easy way to make a better you?
There are so many factors involved in espresso preparation that only a human mind and passionate heart can begin to understand and control its complexity."	Define three areas where you are beautifully complex.

Continued on next page

Chapter 1: Espresso and You, Continued

God definition of you

God made you and has a description of you too.

"¹³For you created my inmost being; you knit me together in my mother's womb. ¹⁴ I praise you because I am fearfully and wonderfully made; your works are wonderful, I know that full well. ¹⁵ My frame was not hidden from you when I was made in the secret place. When I was woven together in the depths of the earth, ¹⁶ your eyes saw my unformed body. All the days ordained for me were written in your book before one of them came to be."

— Psalms 139:13–16 (NIV)

- Describe areas in your life where it is difficult for you to accept that you are fearfully and wonderfully made?

How many?

There are many women impacted by domestic violence around the world. Patterns of abuse in your life can leave a residual impact that defines who we are, what we think and how we react to people, places and things. Let's take a look at some of the facts about abuse and know are not alone.

Continued on next page

Chapter 1: Espresso and You, Continued

Many feel like you do

There are many women who feel the same way you do. They experience the same struggle to overcome and are uncertain where to turn for help and support. You are not alone. Networks of individuals, groups and organizations in your local community are available to help you.

Statistics

It does not matter how much money you have, how much education you have received, what color you are or where you live. Domestic abuse happens in every race, religion, culture and economic group. Note the following domestic violence statistics:[2]

- One out of every three women will be abused at some point in her life.
- Battering is the single major cause of injury to women, exceeding rapes, muggings and auto accidents combined.
- A woman is more likely to be killed by a male partner (or former partner) than any other person.
- About 4,000 women die each year due to domestic violence.
- Of the total domestic violence homicides, about 75% of the victims were killed as they attempted to leave the relationship, or after the relationship had ended.
- Seventy-three percent of male abusers were abused as children.
- Thirty percent of Americans say they know a woman who has been physically abused by her husband in the past year.
- Women of all races are equally vulnerable to violence by an intimate partner.
- On average, more than three women are murdered by their husbands or partners in this country every day.
- Intimate partner violence is a crime that largely affects women. In 1999, women accounted for 85% of the victims of intimate partner violence.
- On average, a woman will leave an abusive relationship seven times before she leaves for good.

Continued on next page

Chapter 1: Espresso and You, Continued

Different types of abuse

Domestic abuse can range from physical, emotional, verbal, financial and sexual behavior.

Often women say, "Well, he never hit me…." Unfortunately, they do not recognize that their "normal" is skewed. They are surviving in relationships that have unhealthy, inappropriate demonstrations of love and anger, and reflect an unhealthy partnership.

Over time what is "normal" shifts and the victim develops coping mechanisms that allow them to survive the abuse. The cycle continues and you begin to cover, excuse, ignore, detach or create other techniques just to survive.

When you finally break free from an abusive relationship, scars remain and new coping mechanisms must be established for your patterns to change.

Chapter Ten of this workbook has detailed information about the characteristics of each type of abuse. You will learn about each type in detail to understand what you endured and what normal should look like.

Continued on next page

Chapter 1: Espresso and You, Continued

Are you being abused?

Physical violence is only one kind of abuse. Answer the following 15 questions; based on your number of "Yes" answers you can better evaluate the severity of your situation:

	Question	Yes	No
1.	Are you blamed whenever things go wrong, cursed or called names?		
2.	Is free time limited to your partner's interest only?		
3.	Do you do more than a fair share of work, paid or unpaid?		
4.	Is your partner a "nasty" drunk or drug user?		
5.	Are you made to have unwanted sex after you've said "no"?		
6.	Do you feel you must ask permission to do things?		
7.	Are you forbidden to use money? Never buy anything for yourself?		
8.	Are you sometimes punished for misbehaving?		
9.	Is it impossible to enjoy outside friendships, due to jealousy?		
10.	In his / her childhood, was your partner or his / her mother abused?		
11.	Does s/he have "Jekyll & Hyde" personality?		
12.	Are you the "butt" of humiliating jokes?		
13.	Is there a scene if you express an opposite opinion?		
14.	Do you "cover" or make excuses for your partner's behavior?		
15.	Do you live in fear of your loved one?		

Continued on next page

Chapter 1: Espresso and You, Continued

Are you sure you're not abused?
(continued)

Tabulate your score. If you have answered yes to:

Score	Action
1 or 2:	Take notice, strive together to improve troubled areas.
3 or 4:	Seriously examine relationships, seek help from qualified source.
4 to 6:	Relationship breaking down, ABUSE is the issue. Joint counseling is not appropriate until FEAR ceases.
7 to 15:	CRISIS INTERVENTION NEEDED! Seek individual help from sources / advocates familiar with abuse issues. Joint counseling is not appropriate.

Source: Domestic Abuse Shelter, Inc., *Are You Sure You're Not Abused?,* (Monroe County, FL: Domestic Abuse Shelter, Inc., 2003).

Action

If you have answered "Yes" to 7–15 of the questions, seek help immediately! You should not deal with this alone. There is a network of Domestic Abuse professionals who can provide counseling, information and resources. Depending on your financial position, much of this care is offered for free, or at low cost, based on your income.

Please seek the proper care and counseling to support you during this time. Call 9-1-1 or the National Domestic Violence Hotline at 1-800-799-7233 to help find resources in your area.

If you do not have a safe computer to use, then you can go to a local library, fire station, police station or church and ask for information. Check the www.strongerthanespressso.com site for resources or call for information.

Continued on next page

Chapter 1: Espresso and You, Continued

Heightened awareness

When you break the cycle, the cycle cannot continue. Understand with an abusive relationship safety is vital. If you are still in your abusive relationship once you react differently the power they have begins to crack.

The risks in your situation are very real. Once the control the abuser has over you begins to diminish or change it becomes a very dangerous time for you. Have a heightened awareness of your surroundings and safety. Be smart and safe. In Chapter Ten we learn more about creating a safety plan or visit www.strongerthanespresso.com for more information.

Connections

When you have spent too much time being alone and isolated; connecting with others is an important part of the healing process.

If you are in a STE class share your phone number with individuals that you feel comfortable with to begin connecting and building your support system. Throughout the week you can send encouraging notes to one another or contact each other when you have a difficult problem to face and need help. Seek out women in your church or community as well. If you are online there are other ways to connect with other women; go to www.strongerthanespresso.com for more information.

"A person standing alone can be attacked and defeated, but two can stand back-to-back and conquer. Three are even better, for a triple-braided cord is not easily broken."

— Ecclesiastes 4:12 (New Living Translation)

Notes:

Chapter 2: Your "Aha" Moment

Purpose

Chapter 2 helps you discover the impact abuse has had on your life and teach you skills to develop personal and Biblical strategies to overcome.

You are jolted awake

For all of us, there is an "aha" moment, line in the sand, epiphany, straw that broke the camel's back, event which occurs in our abusive relationship. In this moment, you recognize the domestic abuse. You finally admit that it is not going to change. It can happen in one flash, one word, one touch, one slap, one hit, one kick, one look, one fight, or one profanity screamed right in your face.

When this moment happens, you can no longer remain ignorant. The vivid reality of your existence becomes clear. Your hope is stripped away, and the "dream talk" you clung to no longer clouds the truth of your reality.

After years of repeated abuse, one day enough is enough. Anywhere, anytime, it can happen. The event leaves you no alternative but to choose something different.

In abusive relationships, you allow the behavior to continue because you hope that the situation will improve. There are times when the relationship is going well, and the "dream talk" soothes your pain. Then in an instant, you are attacked by an emotional machine gun spray. The assault of their verbal bullets shatters your hopes once again.

Once you are jolted awake you are no longer clouded by the truth of your reality, and you see your relationship for what it is. The cycle of abuse and perpetuation of violence is clear and you know you must escape.

It marks the beginning of the journey. You have sustained many hurts of emotional and physical abuse and even struggled to comprehend this behavior as abuse. You want to believe it is normal. Once you begin your awakening, it is very difficult to continue in the same situation. Future events will feel like earthquake aftershocks as you recognize it as domestic abuse. It may be months or years before you have the courage to begin to change your situation.

Continued on next page

Chapter 2: Your "Aha" Moment, Continued

Time to move   The fact that you are reading this workbook means God has activated you to complete His healing now.

Once you are jolted awake, you are never, ever the same.

You know you must move forward, but how?

"Aha" moment   Take time to identify your "aha" moment and discover the impact on your life.

Describe the moment you were jolted awake?

What impact did this event have on you?

What steps do you still need to take to overcome its impact on your life?

Continued on next page

Chapter 2: Your "Aha" Moment, Continued

My jolt awake moment

"My epiphany came as I waited in the small mobile trailer waiting for a free cell phone.

Two weeks prior to this I had been in the emergency room due to being hit in the face by my husband and he had begun to stalk me. I was told that I could get a free cell phone that would call an emergency number if I needed it.

My heart was racing, palms sweating, nauseated, totally terrified that "he" was watching, and had observed me go into this place. Despite what led me there I had not even accepted what I was experiencing was called domestic abuse. I was naïve and ignorant to the term so I didn't realize how it exactly described my situation.

As I waited for a counselor a large poster on a wall caught my attention which changed everything. (The poster had the same questions answered in the previous Chapter Are You Sure You Are Not Abused?)

This was my jolt awake moment!

I had answered "Yes" to all 15 questions. What had become normal to me was actually dangerous. I read and reread the last Action statement, "Crisis Intervention Needed" bewildered and stunned.

My throat tightened, my stomach winched and tears welled up from deep inside; I began to weep in the small, stuffy mobile trailer. At that moment I was jolted awake and finally recognized the severity of my abuse and knew that action had to be taken.

All my relationships before had always ended up at a point similar to this one; I was hurt and broken. This was my normal. It is called abuse. I thought I deserved the abuse.

You mean it isn't my fault?

Continued on next page

Chapter 2: Your "Aha" Moment, Continued

God hears you

God hears you. Even in your darkest hour and in difficult times, God listens to your prayers. Answers to your prayers come in God's timing which is sometimes hard to understand. Over time as you look back it becomes clear what God's plan was and is for your life.

"²¹Praise be to the Lord, for he showed his wonderful love to me when I was in a besieged city.²² In my alarm I said, 'I am cut off from your sight!' Yet you heard my cry for mercy when I called to you for help.²³Love the Lord, all his saints! The Lord preserves the faithful, but the proud he pays back in full.²⁴ Be strong and take heart, all you who hope in the Lord."
                    — Psalms 31:21–24 (New International Version)

Do not be afraid

Once we realize we are in an abusive situation or have just survived one; it is normal to be afraid. Carrying that fear everyday will erode your ability to develop. The fear will deteriorate your growth. Releasing that fear is important to becoming Stronger than Espresso!

"¹³Moses answered the people, 'Do not be afraid. Stand firm and you will see the deliverance the Lord will bring you today. The Egyptians you see today you will never see again.¹⁴ The Lord will fight for you; you need only to be still."
                    — Exodus 14:13,14 (NIV)

Darkness revealed

It is not surprising that eventually you are jolted awake. God has promised us that all darkness will be revealed. God is the light and his brightness will outshine all others.

"If I say, 'Surely the darkness will hide me and the light become night around me,' even the darkness will not be dark to you; the night will shine like the day, for darkness is as light to you."
                    — Psalms 139:11 (NIV)

Continued on next page

Chapter 2: Your "Aha" Moment, Continued

Transform your mind

Now that you know the truth about your relationship; it is time to change! God helps us know that we can be transformed with the renewing of our mind. That is true freedom to think differently about ourselves and our lives.

"Do not conform any longer to the pattern of this world, but be transformed by the renewing of your mind. Then you will be able to test and approve what God's will is – his good, pleasing and perfect will."

— Romans 12:2 (NIV)

"[She demolishes] arguments and every pretension that sets itself up against the knowledge of God, and [she takes] every thought captive to the obedience of Christ."

— 2 Corinthians 10:5 (NIV)

Impact

What is the impact of these scriptures on your life?

What are three things you can begin today to apply this truth in your life?

1.

2.

3.

Continued on next page

Chapter 2: Your "Aha" Moment, Continued

Scripture link

Describe how each scripture impacts you and list ways you can demonstrate the scripture's truth in your life.

Scripture	Impact on You	Ways the Scripture Applies in Your Life
Psalms 31:21–24 (NIV)		
Exodus 14:13, 14 (NIV)		
Psalms 139:11 (NIV)		
Romans 12:2 (NIV)		

Ready, Set, Go   If you keep doing the same 'ole thing, you will keep getting the same 'ole thing. In the next Chapter you begin to explore your emotions and learn ways to replace them with new and refreshing opposites.

Chapter 3: Feelings Assessment

Purpose

The purpose of Chapter 3 is to help you identify your emotions, what actions/ reactions they generate, and how these actions/reactions impact your life. Once these are identified you will create 180 degree opposites and begin replacing the current negative feelings with refreshing new solutions.

Balanced on the Edge of a Knife

"I lived balancing on the edge of a knife. It was years of being with abusers that conditioned me to continually taking the blame for everything. I suffered extreme loneliness and would emotionally detach so that my heart would not be touched. I pushed loved ones away for fear that they might see who I really am and not like me. I did not believe that I was worthy of unconditional love and so history kept repeating itself."

Current Feelings

Finish the following sentence stems:

- My life has become…

  _____

- Normal now seems…

  _____

- I am isolated from …

  _____

- My safe harbor is …

  _____

- The first thing I want to change is …

  _____

Continued on next page

Chapter 3: Feelings Assessment, Continued

Themes

These words are a combination of emotions, actions and the results or impact these feelings can have in your life.

Circle words that describe you:

Figure 2. Emotions, Actions and Results.   Source: Stronger than Espresso, Inc. © 2014.

Continued on next page

Chapter 3: Feelings Assessment, Continued

Themes (continued)

Review the words you circled.

Some of the words will describe an emotion you feel, an action you perform, or a result you receive because of your action or emotions. Try to categorize your circled words as an emotion, an action or a result. Words can be used more than once, and don't worry about getting words in the "right" column. There is no wrong answer. This is to help you start to recognize your emotions, what your actions these create, and the result or impact it causes in your life.

Think of this as a process and move from left to right.

⟶

Feeling / Emotion	Action	Result/Impact
Example: **Anger**	**I shutdown**	**I live behind a plastic smile** and emotionally detach from others.

Continued on next page

Chapter 3: Feelings Assessment, Continued

Your 180

The purpose of this table is to help you create 180 degree opposite solutions.

Take any words listed on the chart on the previous page and create what is the new and refreshing opposite emotion, action or result. The opposite is your 180 degree solution. The first one is done for you as an example.

Complete the table for all your circled words to develop your 180 degree solutions:

180 Feeling / Emotion	180 Action	180 Result
If Anger *the 180 =***Joy**	*For* Shut down = **Open**	*For* Plastic = **Be honest**

Table 1. Emotions, Actions and Results Comparison.   Source: Stronger than Espresso, Inc. © 2014

Continued on next page

Chapter 3: Feelings Assessment, Continued

Expect to change

One day when you feel the piercing arrow of someone's words you will no longer revert to that small unimportant child. A child who wants to run, hide, make it stop, or even fight back.

You have hope for change. With a commitment to completing your emotional journey and a dedication to accept God's love into your life; you will experience a life like never before.

You can have a healthy partner and supportive and loving relationship in the future if you choose. You can break the cycle, make better choices and receive the love and respect you deserve.

God's love can FILL-up areas you have been trying to FEEL-up.

God's love for us is unending and offers true forgiveness.

"[37]Know in all these things we are more than conquerors through him who loved us. [38] For I am convinced that neither death nor life, neither angels nor demons, neither the present nor the future, nor any powers, [39] neither height no depth, nor anything else in all creations, will be able to separate us from the love of God that is in Christ Jesus our Lord."
— Romans 8:37-39 (NIV)

Describe areas you want God to change in your life?

Strength to change

Our hurts are so big and overwhelming at times. There is strength of the almighty God that can carry your burden. Sharing burdens aloud can help you begin to heal.

"I can do everything through him who gives me strength."
— Philippians 4:13 (NIV)

"Therefore, confess your sins to each other and pray for each so that you may be healed...."
— James 5:16 (NIV)

What burdens do you need God to carry right now?

Notes:

Chapter 4: Coping Mechanisms

Introduction

Coping mechanisms could also be described as survival behaviors. They are used to counter our partner's behavior, and often are reaction methods we established years ago in our childhood. Identifying these behaviors will begin your healing process.

Purpose

The purpose of Chapter 4 is to help you identify you coping mechanisms. Self responsibility of your perpetual patterns and reactive behaviors is very important so you can create the steps for conscious change. Accepting God's love and knowing you are worthy is a foundation part of this change taking root.

Shift from normal

When you have been pulled out of normal, it is difficult to know what normal is. Often these relationships start off electric, intense, passionate and we are swept off our feet. Over time the abuse begins to show a little at a time. We make excuses and justify the abuse. This is the beginning to a shift to what becomes a new normal for acceptable behavior in relationships.

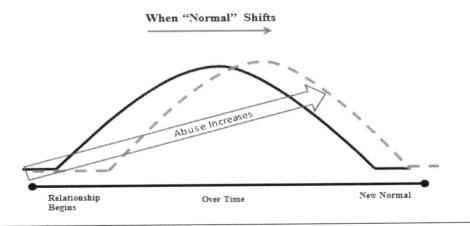

Figure 3. When "Normal" Shifts.   Source: Stronger than Espresso, Inc. © 2014.

In order to grow you must identify your coping techniques to heal.

Continued on next page

Chapter 4: Coping Mechanisms, Continued

Gratefulness

You will be forever grateful that you have been jolted awake, because now God can complete a work in you. There is a way out of the well you have fallen into.

Response

When this shift occurs, we begin to deny, justify, make excuses and shift blame. Often in abusive relationships, we learn to run from, stuff down or hide our emotions. You learn that these are safer responses to confronting those that hurt us. We learn quickly that confrontation leads to danger. We develop techniques to survive including detachment and we learn how to become emotionally numb.

Coping mechanisms

Describe ways that you currently cope with confrontation.

-
-
-

What are the risks if you continue using these methods?

-
-
-

What coping mechanisms would you like to change?

-
-
-

Continued on next page

Chapter 4: Coping Mechanisms, Continued

Take the first step

If there are behaviors you want to change, describe steps you can take to change these behaviors?

Abusers behaviors

Identify behaviors of your abuser that are not healthy.

Describe any behaviors that overlap between you both (be honest)?

What is the risk if you continue your unhealthy behaviors?

What other areas in your life do you transfer those behaviors?

Continued on next page

Chapter 4: Coping Mechanisms, Continued

Share and connect

Have you ever told anyone about your unhealthy behaviors?

If you answered, "Yes," who did you tell? What happened when you did?

If "No," why have you kept it hidden?

Confess to one another

True healing can occur when we confess to one another and receive the full blessing of Jesus.

"Therefore, confess your sins to each other and pray for each other so that you may be healed. The prayer of a righteous man is powerful and effective."
— **James 5:16 (NIV)**

Secrets

You are as vulnerable as your deepest secret. By confessing areas where you are unhealthy, you are released to receive God's mercy.

"[She] who conceals [her] sins does not prosper, but [she who] confesses and renounces them finds mercy."
— **Proverbs 28:13 (NIV)**

What secrets would you like to get rid of today?

Continued on next page

Chapter 4: Coping Mechanisms, Continued

Ask God to help

God reveals vulnerable areas, bad habits or behaviors that need to change.

"...Wash me, and I will be whiter than snow."   **— Psalms 51:7 (NIV)**

"Direct my footsteps according to your word; let no sin rule over me."
    — Psalms 119:133 (NIV)

What is God revealing to you that need to change?

Unlock the potential

Women need to understand the depth of God's love for them. Many of you still feel worthless, invisible, not good enough and you struggle with accepting they are worthy. When a woman finally starts believing she is worthy of God's love she has the a key to unlock her full Stronger than Espresso potential!

God's Promise

He who began a good work in you should complete that work until the finish.

"Be confident in this, that He who began a good work in you will carry it on to completion until the day of Christ Jesus."
    — Philippians 1:6 (NIV)

Continued on next page

Chapter 4: Coping Mechanisms, Continued

Spiritual awakening

One day, after finishing a three-day Christian women's conference, I went to the ocean to swim. During that swim I was surrounded by angels and they were laughing and playing in the water with me. The water turned a fluorescent turquoise. I was surrounded by other people in the water but I saw no one else during this surreal experience. As each wave passed over me, I heard God's voice whispering in my ear, "I love you, and I forgive you. Let it go." I played in the water, laughed and cried washing away years of shame. I felt cleansed surrounded by the love of God and the angels.

When the imagery subsided, I made my way to the shore and lay down on the hot warm sand. With my eyes closed, I was unable to speak and tingled from head to toe. The experience that day filled the hole in my heart. I had personal cravings that could never be satisfied, but they were finally satiated at that moment. Filling that craving was a spiritual experience that transformed me from the inside out.

Since that day, I have made it my priority to surround myself with good people and make healthy choices that protect the beautiful spirit I have. This allows me to walk by faith and trust that God will protect me and shine the lamp on the road I must travel. It was not overnight but my journey began that day. Years now have past, and a strong faith in God has blessed my life. I am healing the pain of the passed and building new pathways from old broken patterns of behavior. Freedom in Him!

Continued on next page

Chapter 4: Coping Mechanisms, Continued

God's grace and love

God's love for you has no limits.

"⁴But because of his great love for us, God who is rich in mercy, ⁵ made us alive with Christ even when we were dead in transgressions – it is by grace you have been saved. ⁶ And God raised us up with Christ and seated us with him in the heavenly realms in Christ Jesus, ⁷ in order that in the coming ages he might show the incomparable riches of his grace, expressed in his kindness to us in Christ Jesus."

— Ephesians 2:4-7 (NIV)

How to accept God's love

After so many years of not feeling worthy of love, it can be difficult to accept God's love.

A simple prayer can release God's blessing and favor over your life. Just say this prayer aloud.

"That if you confess with your mouth, 'Jesus is Lord,' and believe in your heart that God raised him from the dead, you will be saved."

— Romans 10:9 (NIV)

Priestly blessing

Bringing God into your life can release blessings over all areas in your life. This is a wonderful blessing to say daily or when you need relief from a difficult and stressful situation.

"²⁴ The Lord bless you and keep you;
²⁵ May the Lord make his face shine upon you and be gracious to you;
²⁶ the Lord turn his face toward you and give you peace."

— Numbers 6:24-26 (NIV)

Continued on next page

Chapter 4: Coping Mechanisms, Continued

You have strength in God

It can be scary to break away from old behaviors. New emotions of joy and feelings of strength do not feel comfortable. Low self-esteem and past hurts have held you back from growing. Know that you have a strong God and cannot be bullied. With Him in your life you have the strength to conquer any challenge that is presented in your life.

"²The Lord is my rock, my fortress and my deliverer; my God is my rock, in whom I take refuge. He is my shield and the horn of my salvation, my stronghold. ³I call to the Lord, who is worthy of praise, and I am saved from my enemies."

— Psalms 18:2-3 (NIV)

God your protector

No longer will you face a hurt alone. As a child of God you are protected by his covering. This does not mean bad things won't happen to us; it does mean that when they do we can ask for His protection to carry us through the challenge.

"How is your view of your Heavenly Father different than your earthy father?"

"⁸Keep me as the apple of your eye; hide me in the shadow of your wings ⁹ from the wicked who assail me, from my mortal enemies who surround me."

— Psalms 17:8-9 (NIV)

Continued on next page

Chapter 4: Coping Mechanisms, Continued

God's love in your life

Describe how you feel when you envision God's great love for you?

List the benefits you will receive by accepting His love?

What are the risks if you believe that you are not worthy of His love?

What is the first area you want God's love to change in your life?

Get ready. Drink up, you are Stronger than Espresso!

Notes:

Section One Summary

In review

Crafting a perfect you is an art that requires dedication and precision. You have unlimited potential and just by changing your focus you can improve your situation. You were not created to be perfect. Believe how beautifully complex you are. There is no quick and easy way to build a better you, but your desire and passion to improve will carry you through. You have created coping mechanisms as your survival strategy. There is good news; God's love can cover and heal all of the hurts you have experienced and change those coping mechanisms.

If you believe you are suffering from domestic abuse know that you are never alone. There are many resources available to help you, and thousands have experienced the pain and suffering you are facing. Recognizing that you are in an abusive situation is the first step.

Actions

Begin changing your life:

- Identify how you were created to be unique, not perfect, like a cup of espresso.
- Review your responses to the *Are You Being Abused?* Questionnaire and seek the level of intervention suggested.
- Recognize the circumstances and events that have jolted you awake to recognize an abusive situation that must be changed.
- Practice applying your new actions from your 180 degree opposites.
- Review your coping mechanisms and pray for God to give you understanding as to how those can change.
- Accept God's love in your life.

My VIPs

What were the most Valuable Important Points (VIPs) you learned in this Section:

-
-
-

Continued on next page

Section One Summary, Continued

Study	Scripture review of the Section. Use this list for further personal study to understand God's word:

Scripture	Objective	Personal Thoughts
Psalms 139:13–16	Spirituality — love, self-acceptance	
Ecclesiastes 4:12	Connections	
Psalms 31:21–24	Spirituality — love	
Exodus 14:13,14	Self-esteem — confidence	
Psalms 139:11	Spirituality — self acceptance	
Romans 12:2	Forgiveness — grow beyond Self-esteem — achievement	
2 Corinthians 10:5	Self-esteem — acceptance	
Romans 8:37–39	Spirituality — love	
Philippians 4:13	Self-esteem — confidence	
James 5:16	Connections — mentors	
Proverbs 28:13	Forgiveness — release anger Self-esteem — achievement	
Psalms 51:7	Spirituality — love Forgiveness — grow beyond	
Psalms 119:133	Spirituality — self-acceptance	
Philippians 1:6	Self-esteem — confidence	
Ephesians 2:4–7	Spirituality – love	
Romans 10:9	Spirituality – love	
Numbers 6:24–26	Spirituality – love Self-esteem – confidence	
Psalms 18:2–3	Self-esteem – confidence	
Psalms 17:8-9	Self-esteem – confidence	

Section 2: Recognizing Patterns of Behavior

Overview

Introduction

In this Section you perform the exciting task of discovering patterns of behavior, relationship "hooks," and self-destructive choices. Identifying these is the first step to change. Learning your patterns will help you avoid a repeat of past experiences and lead to a happier healthier you.

Contents

This section contains the following topics:

Course Objectives

Upon completion of this Section, you will be able to:

- Identify reoccurring themes in your relationships.

- Demonstrate the ability to change your inner music or self-talk.

- Create new affirmations to speak over your life.

- Define parent-child hooks and the impact they have on your behavior.

- Identify the medical impact resulting from abusive relationships and patterns of abuse you have faced throughout your life.

Notes:

Chapter 5: Reoccurring Themes

Purpose	The purpose of Chapter 5 is to help you identify the reoccurring themes in your life. The reoccurring themes begin as your destructive self-talk. They penetrate your self-esteem, your relationships, your ability to set healthy boundaries, and often restrict your view of your own value. Only by identifying these themes can your alternative self-talk begin to change.
Introduction	In the last chapter we learned about our feelings. This chapter helps you discover your reoccurring themes, what fears you have, and what stumbling blocks exist and any challenges you must confront. Be honest in your self-assessments. When you see your situation for what it is, you can transform. Overcoming denial is the first step to your new life.
The "Usual to go"	You pull open the glass door of your corner coffee shop filling your lungs with air permeated with a thick and pungent aroma of freshly ground dark-roast coffee. The store bustles with early morning activity as you take your place sandwiched in line between busy professionals chattering on cell phones, soccer moms on a mission and a few "grunters" that will not speak or make eye contact until they get that first cup of java. As you wait, your foot taps to the beat of a jazz melody playing through the café sound system. When you hear the coveted sound, "Next," you make eye contact with the barista and stride toward the counter.
	You order, *"Good morning, I will have the usual."*
	The barista smiles, creates your customized coffee creation and says, *"One usual to go."* You grab your "usual" and go about your day.
	A "Barista" is one who has acquired some level of expertise in the preparation of espresso-based coffee drinks. They take your order and create a coffee delight with coffee beans, various methods of steamed milk and other add-ins to the drink.
	They can make endless varieties of drinks, yet they "serve what you order."

Continued on next page

Chapter 5: Reoccurring Themes, Continued

Try something new

Life is a continued repetition of learned patterns of behavior. If you continue to ask for the same thing every day, then you will continue to receive the same outcome. Only when you begin to branch out and try something new can a different outcome occur.

What are the benefits if you tried something new today?

Your desire for change

Complete the following questions:

- List areas in your life where you want to change but you keep trying the same things expecting a different outcome?

- Describe what true freedom from these items would look like?

3-Legged stool

"For years I sat on a three-legged stool. Partners would kick out one of the legs just when I began to succeed. I continued to fall in love with men that were emotionally, verbally, physically and financially abusive. Why?"

What are my patterns?

The first step to any recovery process is to identify where you are right now. Understanding that your brutal reality is your beginning point. No matter how difficult it is to admit.

You must identify your patterns of behavior. This awareness allows you to correct and never say, "Oh, here, I go" again. A skill you must develop is how to identify those reoccurring patterns again in your life, and how to make different choices. Inviting God into your daily life and accepting His divine love will make this process easier. Rest assured that you have been "wonderfully made" by your God and with that mindset you can begin.

Continued on next page

Chapter 5: Reoccurring Themes, Continued

Timing

For everything God has a time and your time is now!

¹ *There is a time for everything, and a season for every activity under heaven:*

² *a time to be born and a time to die,*
a time to plant and a time to uproot,

³ *a time to kill and a time to heal,*
a time to tear down and time to build,

⁴ *a time to weep and a time to laugh,*
a time to mourn and a time to dance,

⁵ *a time to scatter stones and a time to gather them,*
a time to embrace and a time to refrain,

⁶ *a time to search and a time to give up,*
a time to keep and a time to throw away,

⁷ *a time to tear and a time to mend,*
a time to be silent and a time to speak,

⁸ *a time to love and a time to hate,*
a time for war and a time for peace.

— Ecclesiastes 3:1-8 (NIV)

- Describe what season you are in right now?

- Where do you want to be?

- List one thing you can change today to begin moving toward where you want to be.

Remember, every day YOU have a choice of how you will feel and how you will spend your time or energy.

Continued on next page

Chapter 5: Reoccurring Themes, Continued

Purpose

"⁷Ask and it will be given to you, seek and you will find; knock and the door will be opened to you. ⁸ For everyone who asks receives; [she] who seeks finds, and to [her] who knocks, the door will be opened."
— Matthew 7:7–8 (New King James Version)

Have you ever been told God has a purpose for your life? If yes, good for you, but honestly, most of us don't have a clue what our purpose is.

One way to find your purpose is to think of moments, memories, activities or specific settings when you are the happiest. The good news is these activities often represent God's purpose in your life through your unique gifts.

Describe activities or settings when you are filled with joy and peace.

What are three actions you can take to begin incorporating these into your weekly activities?

If you are saying, "I can't do that" remember just ask and you shall receive.

Change

Who is responsible:

- You are the only one who can change your behavior.

- You are not responsible for the behavior and actions of your partner(s).

- You are free to choose any emotion or attitude regardless of your situation.

- Reading God's word daily will help you learn how to make better choices based on His lessons and guidelines.

- Daily prayer time will train you to listen to His blessings over your life.

- Transformation is not a quick fix; it takes time and dedication.

Continued on next page

Chapter 5: Reoccurring Themes, Continued

What, Where, Who

You are a complex person and have had intense relationships. Unraveling them and getting to the core can be difficult. Recognizing themes and understanding their impact in your life is the key to making a change. You can change those themes regardless of how long they have ruled your decision process. Unhealthy behaviors begin early in our lives and our themes are rehearsed responses that you have used to survive.

Have you heard yourself saying things like, "Here I go again" or "No matter how hard I try, it's always my fault."

Describe the reoccurring statements you often say:

-
-
-
-
-
-
-
-
-
-
-
-
-

Continued on next page

Chapter 5: Reoccurring Themes, Continued

What Where Who (continued)

Often when we begin our unhealthy self-talk there are similarities we do not see. When you begin to look at what you are doing, where you are, who you are with and how you feel when these reoccurring statements are going through your head, themes begin to emerge. To identify themes in your statements complete the following table to identify commonalities in people, places and things:

Statement 1	Commonalities
When I say …. (what)	
I am usually …(where)	
I am with… (who)	
It makes me feel…	

Statement 2	Commonalities
When I say ….	
I am usually…	
I am with…	
It makes me feel…	

Statement 3	Commonalities
When I say ….	
I am usually…	
I am with…	
It makes me feel…	

Continued on next page

Chapter 5: Reoccurring Themes, Continued

Words to avoid
Saying words like, "never," "always," "no one" can be damaging to you. These words are not constructive to healthy conversation or healthy conflict resolution. Our words matter. They have power and authority. The Build, Break or Bond.

These statements can:

- Blame others
- Block forgiveness
- Lack hope
- Restrict God's grace from fully working in your life
- Keep you from changing your life

List words that you would like to avoid:

List words you would like to add to have healthier conversations:

Power of your tongue

Be mindful of the words you say. Your tongue is a powerful tool. It can speak praise or it can speak negativity over your life.

"He who guards his mouth and his tongue keeps himself from calamity."
— Proverbs 21:23 (New International Version)

Later in this book, in the Seven Measures of Perfection, Ingredient #5 Power of Your Words, we dig deeper into understanding the role of the tongue in your life.

Fake appearances

"I had a college degree, professional career, came from a middle class background. From the outside it looked like I had the world on a platter. Yet, I chose to surround myself with destructive partners."

Continued on next page

Chapter 5: Reoccurring Themes, Continued

Identify reoccurring themes

Your reoccurring themes should be identified, evaluated, and replaced with God's new themes. Regardless of what you think, God believes you are a masterpiece.

The objective in answering these questions is to help you identify reoccurring behavior. Once you have answered the questions, look for commonalities, similar words, people or events that came up in your answers. Circle or highlight information. Use the table on the following page to record your answers. It may help you see patterns and people in your life that need to change.

The questions may strike a chord or bring up a variety of feelings and emotions. Often when confronted with memories you don't like or recognizing your current reality can be difficult to face. When you hide your shortcomings, you do not allow for them to be cleansed. Be prepared to fully disclose your mistakes and weaknesses.

Be honest. Be descriptive. When you are done, review your answers and identify any consistencies or patterns.

1. How do you react when someone criticizes you in public?

2. Why does it feel like no one understands you?

3. When are you jealous of your mate or describe how your mate's jealousy affects you?

4. When are you kept away from working with others?

5. When do you help others but keep it secret for fear of getting caught?

6. Describe when you feel exhausted, overwhelmed and used?

Continued on next page

Chapter 5: Reoccurring Themes, Continued

**Identify
reoccurring
themes**
(continued)

7. Why do you think others don't help you?

8. Describe where and with whom you feel safe.

9. What relationship problem do you keep repeating over and over, even in different relationships?

10. Are you kept away from your spiritual desires?

11. Imagine a perfect life for you, describe what it is like.

12. Who is always getting upset, hurt, angry or disappointed in you no matter how hard you try?

13. Who do you blame for your unhappiness?

14. Describe things you have done in the past that you are ashamed of?

15. When are you most creative? Confident?

Continued on next page

Chapter 5: Reoccurring Themes, Continued

Identify reoccurring themes

Review your answers and record commonalities found when answering the previous series of questions. The commonalities are themes you can begin to change:

	Emotional Response	People	Activities	Places	Memories
1					
2					
3					
4					
5					
6					
7					
8					
9					
10					

Continued on next page

Chapter 5: Reoccurring Themes, Continued

Learn to Redefine

Now it is time to build on the initial foundation of self-acceptance and love and create I will statements.

Situation	Solution
Example: When someone criticizes me in public I will no longer be hurt and withdrawn.	Example: I will say to that person that I do not appreciate being criticized in public. I also choose not to associate with a person that treats me that way. The next time they invite me out, I can decline.
When...	I will...
When...	I will...
When...	I will...

Continued on next page

Chapter 5: Reoccurring Themes, Continued

Courage

It may be uncomfortable to speak those words right now. Courage is taking the first step. Over time you can practice a little at a time. The courage you have shown is to make a conscious solution to change your automatic response to hurtful behavior; a great first step.

You may be working with your partners at Stronger than Espresso® to connect and heal. You may be working with a counselor, sponsor, or trusted friend. It is important you seek someone to discuss these themes. Pray for God to help reveal ways to change and correct behaviors.

"You can stand up in a little cup!"

You are courageous!

Even though you may be as small and delicate as a dainty teacup or demitasse, you are still strong and can stand up in your little cup!

Relationship patterns

Identifying the patterns you have about love and relationships will help you understand how to evaluate your feelings in more depth. Later in the book we learn more about characteristics of abusive relationships.

Have you ever gotten into a relationship and then somewhere past the endless hours of pillow-talk, the candlelit dinners, the walks in the park, the kissing and other good stuff, that you find yourself saying, "Oh no, here I go again." You realize that you are in another relationship that is just like the last one and now you don't know what to do.

That's great if I am falling in love, but what if I am still married or living with this person?

If you are in a current relationship with someone who is abusing you, then you need to seek help. Abusive relationships do not improve without intervention, counseling and the abuser changing. That can occur, but requires a long period of time. As long as you are in the home and in the abusive relationship – you are in danger of the abuse escalating.

Abuse is not okay. It is against the law.

Continued on next page

Chapter 5: Reoccurring Themes, Continued

Identify relationship trends

Often we need to look at our past to understand what we can do differently in our future. Describe your relationship patterns from your past to identify trends. If you see commonalities in your relationship choices seek wisdom in prayer, talk to other women you can trust and know what is unhealthy for you.

Depending on your circumstances and experiences this information may be very relevant to you or not at all. Glean from the information what can be of use to see any patterns you have had in your life.

Honeymoon Phase:

- What attracts you to someone?

- Describe what "falling in love" is like for you?

- What part of you feels complete when the relationship is new?

- What dreams do you believe about this relationship?

- How much do you trust in the beginning?

Continued on next page

Chapter 5: Reoccurring Themes, Continued

Identify relationship trends (continued)

Friction Phase:

- What incidents occurred that began to change the relationship?

- What are the arguments like?

- Do you feel safe or do you feel afraid when you argue?

- Do you become wrapped up in the "dream" that you forget to ask the hard questions and get surprised by the truth later?

- Did alcohol or drugs play a part in the miscommunication or elevated levels of abuse?

"Oh no, Not Again" Phase:

- Describe what happens when "the honeymoon is over."

- How does this behavior mirror your past relationships?

Intimacy

In-To-Me-See. Sounds like intimacy. Beginning as a child, our relationships define our patterns of intimacy. As we grow older, intimacy can define our relationships.
Describe how your intimacy and sex life has been impacted by abuse?

How does the statement, "Sex is a currency" make you feel?

Continued on next page

Chapter 5: Reoccurring Themes, Continued

Identify trends
(continued)

When the same words pop up in your responses, these emotions and hurts are unique to you. They are your repetitive patterns. These emotions will continue to perpetuate in your relationships unless you make a change.

Look for similarities and list them below:

Relationship name	Courting Style	Emotion	Hurt

Self-check

Ask yourself, why are you drawn to these characteristics? Healthy relationships foster mutual respect, love and nurturing. In the next Chapter we learn about how our behaviors can impact our ability to set boundaries.

Teasing isn't for everyone

"One day my husband started teasing me in a way that really hurt my feelings. He began to do this behavior when we were in front of other people. He would pat my head and say, "good girl" especially in front of other women he was trying to impress. I felt like a fool. Like a dog he was patting me on the head. It was demeaning and he would just laugh at me.

Even when I asked him to stop, he just said, "I'm only teasing" and continued to do it. I got angry because I already told him and he wasn't listening.

When I tried to describe my hurt, humiliation, anger, or frustration, he did not validate my feelings nor take them seriously. He thought it was funny and tried even harder to get others to laugh when he did it to me."

Notes:

Chapter 6: Your Behaviors, Set Boundaries

Introduction

In this Chapter we will first review common coping behaviors and then methods to establish healthy boundaries. Coping behaviors are what we do when handling stressful situations, or ways we avoid conflict. These behaviors are methods you choose to help you cope, survive and process your emotions. Often setting boundaries can be difficult if you do not address these behaviors. Changing these behaviors with healthier patterns will help you begin to practice setting healthy boundaries for yourself.

Purpose

The purpose of Chapter 6 is to help you identify your behaviors that contribute to your inability to set healthy boundaries. Once you realize you have a part in this process, you can begin to choose to think and react differently. Setting healthy boundaries is a simple four-step process to define what you want, communicate those rights, know when those boundaries are crossed and identifying self-sabotage.

Main categories

Coping behaviors are different for everyone. They are done to comfort and ease the pain that we feel. Do you give-up, blame, fight, run, hide? Others might eat, drink, smoke, toke, shop, eat, have sex or spend.

Main categories of coping behaviors detailed in this Chapter are:

1. Codependency
2. Unhealthy relationships
3. Addictions
4. Hyper sensitivity

What if you do not know your coping behaviors? Learn more about each and pray for God to reveal areas in your life that need to be healed.

"Then if my people who are called by my name will humble themselves and pray and seek my face and turn from their wicked ways, I will hear from heaven and will forgive their sins and restore their land. "
— **1 Chronicles 7:14 (NIV)**

Continued on next page

Chapter 6: Your Behaviors, Set Boundaries, Continued

Codependency

Taken advantage

Do others in the house fail to help cook, clean, or assist with chores around the house? Do you feel exhausted and have to "do" everything? Do you feel overcommitted and underappreciated? Are you hurt because no one seems to know or care how you feel?

This behavior is called codependency. Codependents attempt to control others, things and events in lieu of controlling their own feelings. They are afraid of being hurt and rejected by others and they often worry and feel anxious, guilty and afraid. They are loyal and often remain in unhealthy relationships which continue to erode their self-esteem and energy levels.

Your life can be different:

- God made you a vibrant, strong and loving person. He loves you just as you are and did not make you to be compulsive.

- As a woman you often show love to your family by performing daily tasks. Be mindful of your motivation. Are you being fueled by anger, resentment and hurt as you complete daily tasks? If so, find ways to release those emotions.

- You have the right to set your own boundaries. Learn how to set boundaries and do not allow others to compromise them. Later in this Chapter we will learn about setting boundaries.

- Your self-worth is not based on what others believe of you or the tasks you complete.

- If you are feeling overwhelmed, ask for help.

- You do not need to be a martyr, miserable and silent.

Answer the following:

Which people in your life take advantage of you?

What tasks do you want them to do for themselves?

Continued on next page

Chapter 6: Your Behaviors, Set Boundaries, Continued

Overwhelmed

Do you feel like you are a slave? Do you feel no one notices you or cares about your feelings? Do you feel exhausted because you must get everything finished? The harder you work the more empty you feel. No one sees your pain and how you suffer. You often feel that if only you could do more or try harder. This is a form of codependent behavior. Feeling codependent is a coping mechanism. It requires you to work toward creating a new response alternative.

There is freedom:

- You have the right to set your own limits.

- If you are not allowed to have rest when you are weary, or freedom from error, then it is not a healthy relationship.

- God made you a beautiful woman. You have the right to accomplish what you can and cannot without punishment.

- Giving our burdens to God will lighten your load and release anxiety.

" [28]Come to me, all you who are weary and burdened, and I will give you rest. [29]Take my yoke upon you and learn from me, for I am gentle and humble in heart, and you will find rest for your souls. [30]For my yoke is easy and my burden is light."

— Matthew 11:28–30 (NIV)

Answer the following:

What would happen if you didn't get everything done?

What is the one thing you could stop doing today to ease your burden?

Tired

"I am tired of being a chameleon to fit in and find love and approval. My gift, my life, must not be wasted. My purpose will unfold if I am true to self. I need to stop being afraid."

Continued on next page

Chapter 6: Your Behaviors, Set Boundaries, Continued

Personal resources

Do people always borrow money and never pay it back? Is it difficult to say "No," even if you are unable to financially do so? Are you often hurt after helping someone because they act dependent and have a level of expectation versus just appreciating your generosity?

Sometimes you think that way because you are a Christian. You are doing the right things to help others. Yes, we are supposed to help one another, but not when it becomes part of an unhealthy pattern. If you feel anxiety, pressure, anger, resentment, frustration or worry, these are signs you are sharing resources as a part of an unhealthy pattern to control and receive acceptance.

Here are some tips:

- Pure and simple—Stop it. This is the hardest step to take. You might say, "But I can't." "The truth is you can." If you feel you can't just stop, then your motivations need to be evaluated.

- It is very important to help others in your life, but you must be in a position to do so first. You must first put your oxygen mask on before helping others. Take care of yourself, your family, your tithe first.

- You need to be honest as to why you are helping someone. Is your motive an attempt to make yourself "lovable" or indispensable to them in an effort to make them "need" you? Do you feel guilty if you don't help?

- Why do they always need to borrow or take from you? If you say No are they able to survive? Have you ever considered God is teaching them during a time of hardship? Spending time with God daily will help you be able to discern God's direction for you and how much and to whom you should direct your resources.

- By lending them money, are you enabling an alcohol or drug dependency? What are their reoccurring patterns that are unhealthy for them? You are loved just as you are, you do not need to "give" anything away to be deserving of the love of others.

- Pray and ask God how you should distribute your finances. It is all his money anyway. Once you allow God to move in your financial realm, you will see his blessings in that area.

Continued on next page

Chapter 6: Your Behaviors, Set Boundaries, Continued

People pleaser

Have you ever been told you are a "people pleaser"?

When you were younger, being a people pleaser was a good quality; you were told you were very nice and always willing to help others. This is a coping pattern of behavior that is created as a child.

Now that you are grown you believe that it is important for you to continue to make people happy. This is an unhealthy need to seek approval from others, and can leave you feeling empty, exhausted and out of control.

You are disappointed in others but feel you can't let them down. Even if it hurts you. You become frustrated when those close to you are not happy. So you just try harder. You believe if you could just make them happy, then life would be easier and things would finally go smoothly.

This is codependent behavior and is not healthy:

- Your partner, family or friend is responsible for their own happiness. You believe that if only you could get everything finished, or get things "just right" they would finally be happy. You are making your happiness dependent on their moods or degree of happiness.

- You are a beautiful child of God just as you are. You do not need approval from anyone and you are responsible for your own happiness.

- Learning that you are not responsible for the happiness of someone else is the place to start. Until you can accept that fact, you will continue to be caught up in this cycle.

What is the worst thing that could happen if you stopped trying to please everyone?

Scurry to placate

"I would drop whatever I was doing and scurry to placate any of his demands. He would be on my heels screaming at me, so I would work hard to just make him stop yelling. It was conditioning. He would scream and his needs would be met. He got the attention and control he desired. I got him to stop yelling. It was a tragic, unhealthy cycle."

Continued on next page

Chapter 6: Your Behaviors, Set Boundaries, Continued

Unhealthy Relationships

Magnet for controlling people

Do you always end up with controlling, selfish, abusive lovers, friends, and coworkers? Are you not sure how it happens? It never starts out that way, but before you know it, they are controlling every move you make. Relationships start like a whirlwind, full of excitement and perfection. Over time you lose control and left empty, exhausted and emotionally sucked dry.

It doesn't have to be that way:

- If you are currently married to an abusive person and living in the same home, you need to seek professional help. Understand the severity of the situation and make sure you are safe. Making changes while in the home can escalate abuse. Contact a local women's shelter or seek the advice of a qualified counselor as you begin to make changes.

- When meeting new people, follow these steps:
  1. Pray specifically that God will bring you a healthy mate.
  2. Educate yourself on abusive warning signs.
  3. Learn to trust your instincts, and no matter how wonderfully you have been "swept off your feet," take it slow.
  4. Learn the signs; heed them, with no exceptions.
  5. Do not fool yourself and make excuses when you see concerning behavior.
  6. Be ready to walk away from anyone who is potentially abusive or dangerous to you.
  7. Conduct a background check.

- For coworkers and friends you need to:
  1. Recognize that their behavior with you is unhealthy.
  2. Inform them you want the specific item to change.
  3. Keep to the facts, do not become emotional.
  4. Allow them to respond. If they throw out a sidetrack, return back to the point. Blame and disrespect are their problem.

Continued on next page

Chapter 6: Your Behaviors, Set Boundaries, Continued

**Relationships
highs and lows**

Do your relationships always have highs and lows? Do they start out great, then something happens and you are back where you started, fighting and in another broken relationship.

When you are uncertain about what sets off the anger and erratic behavior in another person, you operate from a position of fear. This leaves you trying to control areas you can, because you are unable to manage their emotions. It becomes overwhelming and unmanageable. Often you wish things could be stable long enough for you to get a handle on things.

Healthy relationships have changes of emotions too. They are different because they can be tied to past events or consistent behavior patterns. Partners don't live in fear or try to control the other's moods; they may be surprised once in a while when they have a bad day or get upset about an issue. Unhealthy people leave you confused and do not take responsibility for maintaining their own highs and lows. When they go out of bounds, they blame and never accept the responsibility. A few tips to consider:

- Your happiness is your responsibility. Ask God to fill you and sustain your joy. His supply has no limits.

- You have the ability to make your happiness a constant state not subject to the ups and downs of life or another person's mood swings.

- If you are on their "roller coaster," you are in their game. Step out of the game to begin healing. This can seem almost impossible at first, but trust in God for help. Turn your focus on him and through prayer ask him to sustain your emotions.

- You must build a healthy, safe haven in your heart and mind where you repeat positive words, despite the chaos. This buffer protects your happiness regardless of the mood swings of others.

- Evaluate why your happiness is dependent on others.

- Construct a safe network of friends, family, church, connect groups.

"[6]Humble yourselves, therefore, under God's mighty hand, that he may lift you up in due time. [7] Cast all your anxiety on him because he cares for you."

— 1 Peter 5:6–7 (NIV)

Continued on next page

Chapter 6: Your Behaviors, Set Boundaries, Continued

Don't like my partners friends

Do you not like the friends or associates that your partner brings around the home and family?

If you are still in the relationship, you may not be able to safely say what you think. Remember that only abusive relationships leave you in situations where you have NO right to choose or speak up.

Consider this:

- Trust your instincts. If someone gives you a bad feeling, you don't have to be around them.

- You have the right to choose and the right to speak up and say what you want and don't want.

- Keep praying and focusing on being freed from these associates and a time will come when you are free to speak up.

Drags me down

Do you wish your partner would stop causing you all this pain so you could feel better?

Have you considered:

- You are responsible for your state of mind or emotional well-being.

- When you blame others you give up the control to change and manage your own behavior.

- Remove blame from your actions, thoughts and words. When you do this, you are free because you have claimed back control of your emotional state. Change begins in you.

Chapter 6: Your Behaviors, Set Boundaries, Continued

Addictions

Addictive behaviors

What drives your behavior? Is it: food, sex, alcohol, drugs, spending money, anger, rebellion, control, anxiety, perfectionism, fear or something else? What unhealthy behaviors do you choose to attempts to fill-up your emptiness inside?

All of these behaviors can be addictive. With any addictive behavior you are left feeling ashamed and disappointed. You feel weak and this increases negative thoughts. Self-destructive behaviors can lead to more depression and disappointment:

- You must find new friends and a new way to have fun or relax! God is big enough to fill those empty spaces inside.

- If you are brave enough to admit that you struggle with alcohol or drugs, you are beginning the road to success. The problem with alcohol and drugs is that when you "do it" you don't see it as a problem. Once you are free, you will be able to look in from the outside and you will be amazed at the dependency and hook it has on you. Even those that say, "I choose to drink. I never get drunk, but I enjoy a little drink each day to take the edge off. I like my wine to unwind after a hard day's work." Just try to stop 100% for a couple of weeks and see if you struggle. You might be surprised how many reasons and situations you think you have to drink.

- If you surround yourself with individuals that use alcohol, drugs or other addictive behaviors as a habit, you will continue to struggle in that area. Replace the desire to escape into something new. God will show you the way to become free.

- Work with the Stronger than Espresso® program in your area to understand how God's love can replace your hurts with healing.

- Pray to God that He will reveal your bad habits.

"Direct my footsteps according to your word, let no sin rule over me."
— Psalms 119:133 (NIV)

Continued on next page

Chapter 6: Your Behaviors, Set Boundaries, Continued

Can't stop contacting them

Do you find it difficult, almost unbearable to not call the abuser or respond when they contact you? Do you feel you have to, so they don't get angry?

The need to be constantly in touch is a part of codependency and addictive behavior. This is a form of control by both parties and is not healthy behavior.

- You do not need to text, call, check on or check in multiple times a day. This is a type of addictive behavior. Continuing with this behavior keeps you as a puppet on a string and you come when you are called.

- If you believe that you "must" contact them with answers or "check in" so they don't get angry, this is abuse and it is not safe for you. Contact a local women's program or Stronger than Espresso® to link you with support and safety resources in your area. Follow the instructions to create a safety plan.

- Social networking sites can be a platform to send notes, monitor behavior and thrive on the movements of each party. It can very quickly become out of balance. Review your motivations to evaluate what drives your need to interact and to what level.

- Just as with any addictive behavior you need to understand why you do it.

- Spend that time praying and asking God what you should do.

- Talk to a trusted friend, counselor, sponsor, victim's advocate or Stronger than Espresso® representative to discuss your feelings and work to overcome this issue.

- The abuser could use the number of times you contacted them as a case to have your Injunction or stalking charges dropped from the court system.

Continued on next page

Chapter 6: Your Behaviors, Set Boundaries, Continued

Hypersensitivity: Self-doubt, anxiety, blame, shame

Trust your instincts

Do you feel that your emotions are out of balance? Are you frustrated because you cannot control or understand the abuser's reactions? Are you overwhelmed by self-doubt, anxiety, blame and shame for mistakes that are not your fault?

This perpetual pressure creates hypersensitivity. These periods of hypersensitivity often don't have any "down" time. You are always on edge or walking on eggshells so you never have time to stop and listen to what your own instincts are telling you.

Realize that your life, your relationships, and your surroundings are out of control. When you find yourself out on your own after the abusive relationship is over, you can try to create similar chaos because it is something you are accustomed to. If you find yourself drawn to overspend, overeat, or overdo in any area, check your motivations. If you choose to make unhealthy choices instead of healthy ones, make sure you are not depriving yourself of the goodness you deserve.

Trusting God comes first. When you trust Him you can trust yourself. Learning to trust God can be a difficult lesson. He will guide you in the ways you need to go:

- "If it is good for you, then it is okay, if it is not, don't do it."

- Trust your gut instincts and listen to your inner wisdom.

- You can choose how you spend your time and the decisions you make. If these are good choices for you —it's okay, if it's not a good choice for you —don't do it.

"And those who know Your name will put their trust in you; For You, Lord, have not forsaken those who seek You."

— Psalms 9:10 (New King James Version)

Continued on next page

Chapter 6: Your Behaviors, Set Boundaries, Continued

Lack of respect

Do you not like the way people treat you? Do you feel disrespected and used most of the time?

You have grown accustomed to disrespect and may not feel you have value. The reality of what is appropriate behavior has become so confused that you rarely know any more what "normal" looks like. When your self-esteem is low, it is difficult to expect self-respect.

Respect is defined as, "Deferential esteem felt or shown towards a person; heed or regard; polite messages or attentions; regard with deference or esteem; avoid interfering with or harming; treat with consideration; refrain from offending." [3]

Self-respect is created within:

1. You must believe you are worthy of respect or you will not receive it.

2. You set the standards for how others will treat you. This is a very difficult item to change when you have been mentally transformed in an abusive relationship.

3. You deserve this type of treatment, from yourself, and especially from those closest to you.

4. You decide your self-treatment and habits relative to the amount of sleep, healthy food choices, ample water intake, and daily exercise. Make sure you love yourself and others will follow.

5. God - He loves you just as you are.

Receiving respect from others:

1. Begin to establish how you want others to treat you.

2. Ask God to help you overcome codependency behaviors.

3. Learn how to say "No." It can be difficult at first. You have been conditioned that love and acceptance are given only with good behavior. What is the risk if you don't learn to say No and spend the rest of your life hurting?

4. When you treat yourself with respect, others will follow. Work with a counselor, sponsor, friend or mentor to help.

Continued on next page

Chapter 6: Your Behaviors, Set Boundaries, Continued

Fight or flight

As humans we are designed with a natural "fight or flight" response to protect us from danger. Unfortunately, in abusive relationships the "fight or flight" response switch is left in the "on" position and has a significant health impact. Answer the following questions:

- When you get angry, embarrassed or frustrated how do you respond?

- When you have tried to stand up for your rights does it cause arguments and create more problems?

- Do you "run" away (emotionally and/or physically) to deal with your hurt feelings?

- Do you stuff everything inside and say nothing?

- What is the risk if you keep pretending on the outside that everything is okay, but you are breaking apart on the inside?

Chapter 6: Your Behaviors, Set Boundaries, Continued

Fight or flight
(continued)

There is hope in changing this behavior. God reminds us to be anxious for nothing and his peace will be enough.

When you feel a "fight or flight" response, learn to "Walk away versus run away." Choose to move away from a specific person or situation to collect your thoughts so you do not receive or strike out in anger.

This reaction is different than what many of us have learned to do which is to "run away." When you run away, you are continuing the cycle of abuse; therefore, reinforcing that you do not have the right to say "No." You may "run away" into glasses of wine, a destructive night out with friends, or into the kitchen to bang pots and pans saying you are fine. You could mutter statements of anger, toy with suicidal thoughts and endure the pain because our hurts are deep and unresolved.

Sustaining these behaviors is very destructive and will not offer you the peace that God is wishing over your life.

When you are first learning the walk away versus run away, you must expect to make some mistakes, but keep trying. You may feel like a two-year old having a tantrum in your own mind, saying *"I want to run!" "No, you must be an adult." "No! I want to run!"* or full of foot-stomping, crying, and folding arms.

This process is normal and must be completed to make it through to the other side. The outcome is well worth it. Keep a journal of what triggers, how you react, and how you would have liked to react. Construct new pathways of behavior so you can choose a different response in the future. Discuss your findings with other group members in your Stronger than Espresso® class to learn new ways to respond to similar choices.

"[6] Be anxious for nothing, but in everything by prayer and supplication, with thanksgiving, let your requests be made known to God; [7]and the peace of God, which surpasses all understanding, will guard your hearts and minds through Christ Jesus. "

— Philippians 4:6,7 (NKJV)

Continued on next page

Chapter 6: Your Behaviors, Set Boundaries, Continued

Blame

Do you describe your partner's behavior as childish, mean, vulgar, inappropriate, humiliating, embarrassing, hurtful, and painful? Do you try to justify their behaviors by stating how factors such as: sleep deprivation, alcohol, or stress contributed to their lack of self-control?

When you justify someone's behavior, you are not requiring them to be responsible for their actions. "Normal" individuals don't melt down on you at the drop of a hat. Once you begin to see the childish behavior of the abuser you will be amazed how obvious it is. You do not have to be treated that way nor are you responsible for their actions.

You are only responsible for your own actions and not to blame for any abuse:

- If you think you have been doing something too much — stop.

- If you need sleep — try to find a way to get some.

- If you are stressed — begin praying that God gives you all the strength you need to find your way out of this valley.

- Reflect on your God given purpose — try to apply some of those activities which will reduce stress.

Continued on next page

Chapter 6: Your Behaviors, Set Boundaries, Continued

Feel ashamed

Have you ever felt:

- Ashamed of things you have done in the past and actions you continue to do?

- Out of control even when you know things are bad for you?

- You are crazy or need help?

Once you have been saved by God's grace, you can let shame go:

- You are a beautiful child of God. You are human, and humans make mistakes. Ask God to forgive the mistakes you have made. That is why he died for us.

- Yet, you have the power to grow beyond what you have been. Let the Shame go.

- God's slates are clean. The only one keeping a record is you.

- Decide those items you want to change, and change them in your everyday actions.

- Do not spend your energy worrying about what you have done — spend your time and energies identifying the person you want to be.

- Decide to either rebuild any relationships you have broken or recognize that they were unhealthy and seek out new ones. Be honest with yourself, make changes and let go of your shame.

"For with the heart one believes unto righteousness, and with the mouth confession is made unto salvation. [11] For the Scripture says, Whoever believes on Him will not be put to shame...[13] For, whoever calls on the name of the Lord shall be saved."

— Romans 10:9–13 (NKJV)

Continued on next page

Chapter 6: Your Behaviors, Set Boundaries, Continued

Introduction to Establishing Boundaries

When you have low self-esteem, setting boundaries can be difficult and even an abstract concept. Setting boundaries is setting limits on what you want and what you feel comfortable with. It is redefining the "hooks" that get you and reestablishing a new framework of what is acceptable behavior. In the remainder of this Chapter we discuss more detail about how to set boundaries. You have the right to speak up and say what you really want. *Really?* Really!

You have rights

This is the beginning step to setting personal boundaries and it will be foreign to you. You have "stuffed down" your own ideas, thoughts, pains and frustrations for years. Perhaps you learned early on in life that if you spoke your mind, the response would be anger and pain. Understand it is okay to have unexpected outcomes while you transition, but don't be easily discouraged. Keep practicing. Healthy people will begin to react differently to you. Unhealthy people will become frustrated because they can no longer control you. Their reaction is your witness to stop associating with them.

Describe areas in your life where you want someone to stop doing something that makes you feel uncomfortable?

You need to know what your boundaries are, and what you want in order to communicate them to others.

When you set boundaries, keep your statements focused on the facts not your emotions. Speak up and say what you really want. You **must** keep centered on love and centered in your faith and believe in your self-development pathway. Take it slow and gently shift your own view of yourself and the others around you. It will be feel strange to you and odd at first for those around you.

Expect some resistance to change. However, if you make these adjustments and you do not feel safe or fear that harm will come to you, you must seek professional help.

Continued on next page

Chapter 6: Your Behaviors, Set Boundaries, Continued

Don't quit

To reap the full result, you must commit to stay the course no matter what. You have the power to choose how you expect to be treated by others. This change does not happen overnight, but you transform over an extended period of time.

About you

Welcome to the next stage of the new you. It is time to define your personal rights and be able to communicate those rights and boundaries to others. This can be a very difficult time, as many of you have given up who you are to please others and survive your current situation.

You might have forgotten that you really do like: country music, B movies, fried seafood or romance novels, but stopped because your partner didn't approve.

In the past you may have never cracked jokes because you were called stupid, now you have learned you have a great sense of humor. Enjoy these revelations.

List a few things you recently learned about yourself:

-
-
-

Building boundaries

Building boundaries is a four step process:

1. Define how you want to be treated.
2. Learn to communicate those rights.
3. Communicate with others that boundaries are being crossed.
4. Recognize when you sabotage or violate your own boundaries.

Be aware of individuals from your past and begin to communicate to them what behavior is now acceptable or not acceptable to you. If they do not listen or will not change, then they need to remain in your past and you must move beyond them and let them go.

Continued on next page

Chapter 6: Your Behaviors, Set Boundaries, Continued

You have the right

I have the Right

- To love
- To laugh
- To sing
- To dance
- To giggle
- To wiggle
- And to be happy

I have the Right

- To say no
- To be alone
- To set a boundary
- To not be hurt
- To worship and walk by faith
- To trust those closest to me

I have the Right

- Because I am lovable!
- Because I am great!
- Because I am smart!
- Because I am absolutely perfect just the way I am.
- Because I am a perfect child of God!
- Because I love myself just as I am!

I have the Right!   I have the Right!   I have the Right!

Continued on next page

Chapter 6: Your Behaviors, Set Boundaries, Continued

Define your boundaries

Step 1. Define how you want to be treated.

Define how you want to be treated. This can be hard for you — that's okay.

Here are some examples of things you have the right to:

- Communicate openly and honestly without fear of being judged or ridiculed.

- Live without fear of being pushed, shoved, slapped, kicked or choked.

- Share your innermost feelings, dreams, thoughts, failures and successes without fear.

- Have your own interests, ideas and friendships.

- Have your emotional needs met through affections, kindness, caring, equality and respect.

- Share in major and minor decision making with your partner.

- Decide how and when to have sex.

- Freedom, to be yourself.

Source: Domestic Abuse Shelter, Inc., *Your Rights, You Have the Right To….* (Florida Keys, FL).

Now, list rights you want to have:

-

-

-

Continued on next page

Chapter 6: Your Behaviors, Set Boundaries, Continued

Learn to communicate your rights

Step 2. Learn to Communicate your Rights.

One of your basic human rights is the right to say, "No." Unfortunately, when you are in an abusive relationship, you have been conditioned that saying "No" is not a safe thing to do. When you have tried to say, "No" in the past, you learned very quickly the negative ramifications on you or your children. Instead you become conditioned, learning the correct responses, so as not to be hurt.

What exactly does it mean to set up boundaries? Setting up boundaries is simply communicating how others are allowed to treat you, and being able to safely say "No" when you feel uncomfortable with another person's behavior.

Do you find it difficult to say "No?" Many of us struggle with confrontation in various situations and need to understand why we are unable to say "No." There is a difference to choosing not to say "No," versus being unable or so uncomfortable that you cannot. When you accept the horrendous gift your mother-in-law gave you for your wedding, or the fruitcake your coworker gives each year, you may choose to grin and bear it and accept the gift graciously. These situations are different. When your boundaries are trampled, morals violated or personal desires disregarded, you can and should say "No."

When you find yourself unable to say "No" to your husband, lover, co-worker, boss, children, neighbor, friend or family member, you lose control over your ability to manage your life.

If you do not feel safe to say "No," anger, fear, and resentment can bottle up. Your partner continues to not be happy or satisfied with their life. You want to make your partner happy and feel responsible for their moods. You try harder to please them, even when you choose behaviors that you do not want to do. When they remain unhappy or not satisfied you feel like a failure. The vicious cycle leaves you emotionally empty because you have no boundaries for what you want to do or do not want to do. The effort used to bottle and maintain your intense emotions is physically exhausting. Without a healthy release and support system you remain full of resentment and anger which is dangerous to your emotional and physical health.

Continued on next page

Chapter 6: Your Behaviors, Set Boundaries, Continued

Communication Tools

Often our emotions are generated because we do not have healthy communication tools in place.

A VERY effective communication tool is to state to the other party.

When you...

I feel... (this needs to be a word describing an emotion)

I want...

As simple as this sounds, being able to explain exactly what happened that bothered you, specifically state what you feel about the incident, and what you want the other party to do instead is a form of verbal freedom! It saves so much time versus the round and round we go arguments, isolation, detachment, rehearsal and so on. This tool can be used by adults, teens and kids.

When an event happens we are triggered with an emotional response. If we do not have a healthy way to identify how we feel and share with the other person it sets off coping behaviors. These coping behaviors can become old hurts, habits and hang-ups we have become so accustomed to in our lives.

Using this communication technique takes some getting used to. The best way to use this tool is to write down what you are feeling ahead of time. Sounding out your emotions in a logical frame of mind usually works more effectively on the other party. Many times we have stuffed or ignored our emotions and when we finally do speak our mind it never comes out as good as we planned.

Chapter 6: Your Behaviors, Set Boundaries, Continued

When are you unable to say no?

It is common for abuse survivors to have difficulty saying "No." This is also a symptom of codependent behavior; an unhealthy coping mechanism.

Commons items where women struggle saying "No":

- Abuse / harassment.
- Controlling behaviors.
- Doing something you don't want to do.
- Doing favors for others: rides, homework, chores.
- Forced to go places you don't want to go.
- Intimate touching that makes you uncomfortable.
- Lending money.
- Medical procedures.
- Sex — unwanted or in an unwanted way.
- Spending time with people who treat you badly.
- Using alcohol or drugs when others around you use them.

Source: Women in Distress of Broward County, Inc., *Emotional Boundaries* (Fort Lauderdale, FL:Women In Distress of Broward County, Inc., 2003).

Describe situations in your life where you wish you could say "No."

Continued on next page

Chapter 6: Your Behaviors, Set Boundaries, Continued

When are you unable to say no? (continued)	Describe what it would look like if you could take control and say "No" without getting hurt or a negative consequence.
Danger saying "No"	What if I am in danger if I say "No." If you are ever in danger call 9-1-1.
	What are your risks if you did say "No" in these situations?
Learn to communicate your rights clearly to others	Instead of just saying, "No," to someone, have you ever pretended to not be home?
	Have you every avoided someone just so you would not have to confront or tell them what is on your mind?
	Have you ever made up an excuse or fabricated a story?
	This avoidance behavior is common, but is a bad habit and something you want to change.
	Healthy relationships and healthy people know they have the right to say "No." When you avoid or are too frightened or uncomfortable, you sabotage your own growth and perpetuate additional violations of self.
	At first, saying "No" can be very uncomfortable, and you will struggle with your desire to not hurt anyone. By growing through that fear and period of discomfort it will free you up in the future to accept or turn away any behavior that you do not want.
	Stating or writing out your responses in the format *When you... I feel... I want...* will allow you to identify the source or event, allow you to communicate your emotions and explain what you want from the other party.

Continued on next page

Chapter 6: Your Behaviors, Set Boundaries, Continued

Learn to communicate your rights clearly to others
(continued)

Tips to follow:

1. When you set boundaries keep your statements focused on the facts not your emotions. State the facts calmly and directly. Do not lead with emotions.

2. Say what you want. Speak kind words; keep your voice calm.

3. Remember to keep love in your heart and mind as you speak. Pray for the person before you speak to them or call a friend to pray with you before you call. Stay centered on love and pathway to peace.

4. Stay focused on the facts. Do not be allowed to be manipulated into an argument or match of wills by your statement. If this occurs, be polite, excuse yourself and try again another time. You might also be confronted with a sidetrack.

Sidetracks are attempts to derail the conversation. A sidetrack can include: tears, blame or anger. Individuals can also shut down, blow up, or give intellectual responses. They are natural human responses to avoid the conversation and are very common. If you see a sidetrack stick to the facts. Do not let it change the course of your discussion. At times, you may have to give a break and return to the conversation when the other party is ready to listen.

Continued on next page

Chapter 6: Your Behaviors, Set Boundaries, Continued

Just Say "No"

Step 3. Communicate with others when boundaries are crossed.

It can be hard to tell someone when a boundary has been crossed.

How many times should we try to share boundaries with those around us? If we realize that we get the same results two, three and even four times after we have shared we don't like something; you need to decide if this person is good for you or not.

Describe a circumstance that you are currently avoiding, such as: a nosy family member, a co-worker that continuously bothers you or a neighbor that is always borrowing $20 when you too are struggling financially.

List each circumstance in detail and write a description of what you will say to this person. Remember, you do not need to justify your No.

> Here's an Example: Neighbor: *"Can I borrow $20? We don't get paid until Friday."*
>
> You: *"No, I am not able to lend you $20."*
>
> Neighbor: *"Come, on, the baby really needs milk and we will pay you back."*
>
> You: (This neighbor has never paid you back in the past. They always have money for cigarettes and alcohol and borrow for their baby's milk. You have been angered by this practice for months, but when they press you - you always just give in.) *"That is a shame but I cannot help you."*
>
> Neighbor: *"Look I really don't know what I will do if you don't help me? It's for the baby, not me."* (Notice the guilt?).
>
> You: *"Unfortunately, I can't help you."*

Use this area to record scripts saying, "No."

Continued on next page

Chapter 6: Your Behaviors, Set Boundaries, Continued

Characteristics of assertion

Assertiveness is taking responsibility for a relationship and being able to communicate what you want:

1. You are entitled to courtesy, dignity and respect.

2. By not communicating what you want, you encourage the same behavior. To stop the behavior you need to tell the person you do not want this behavior to continue.

3. Not letting others know how you feel or what you think denies them the opportunity to change.

4. "Being polite out of fear of being offensive and hiding one's discontent with the situation or the behavior of the other, is a sure way of either destroying a relationship or preventing one from really forming." [4]

5. Allowing this frustration and resentment to build up, can cause emotional and physical damage to you.

6. You have the right to express yourself, as long as you do not violate the rights of someone else.

7. Strive to be able to communicate your feelings and desires without feeling blame, shame or guilt when you say "No."

8. Being assertive can be uncomfortable at first, but will get easier with practice.

9. There is a difference between feeling uncomfortable and feeling safe. If you do not believe it is safe for you to speak a different opinion or assert your beliefs than you are in an abusive relationship. Seek professional help first from a local women's shelter or licensed counselor to ensure your safety is the number one concern.

Continued on next page

Chapter 6: Your Behaviors, Set Boundaries, Continued

Be assertive

Aggressive and assertive are not the same. Assertiveness states the facts without being pushy or out of control. When you are new at setting boundaries you may explode with words or emotions because they have been shoved down for years. When you get your voice —you want to shout it out! Be mindful of your tendency to overstate your boundaries at first. Hang in there — it's a process.

Answer the following questions:

- Describe situations where you do not express your feelings.

- How do you feel when you do not speak up?

- What are the risks if you stood up for yourself?

- What actions can you take to communicate to this individual how you wish to be treated?

Tread lightly

The communication techniques you learn and apply are very important and vital to developing a new you. When you speak to others state information as a matter of fact. Keep emotions out of your statements. You have repressed emotions for so long this opportunity to speak-up can feel very good. Do not believe that this new-found freedom to communicate is a license to unleash your repressed anger. Bombarding those around you in rude or abrupt ways can create damage you will need to repair down the road.

Continued on next page

Chapter 6: Your Behaviors, Set Boundaries, Continued

How others respond to you

Evaluate the response of others when you begin to gently say "No" and create boundaries. This will be something new for many people close to you. They will notice something different. How do they react:

- Do they get angry?

- Do they act hurt?

- Do they claim you don't love them?

- Do they blame you?

- Do they make you feel guilty?

These responses are their coping mechanisms to unresolved issues and are not your responsibility.

Keep connected to a mentor, coach, counselor, sponsor, friend, or accountability partner to discuss how these small attempts progress. That will keep you focused on why you are changing regardless of their response to you.

Overcome self-sabotage

Step 4. Recognize when you sabotage or violate your own boundaries.

When you do not respect yourself, others will not respect you. Respect yourself:

1. Take care of yourself. Make sure to eat, exercise, rest, socialize and relax.
2. Surround yourself with positive sounds, sights, and people. Avoid negative influences.
3. Avoid all behaviors, people or substances you have used to medicate your emotional pain in the past.
4. Be mindful of your self-talk and keep it positive. Be aware of negative self-thoughts and push them out of your mind.
5. Be realistic about yourself and others.
6. Avoid your own destructive patterns of behavior. Admit they exist and expect the same destructive outcome if you make the same choices.

Continued on next page

Chapter 6: Your Behaviors, Set Boundaries, Continued

Solutions to overcome self-sabotage

Being prepared can help you overcome self-sabotaging behaviors. Answer the following questions:

- Taking care of yourself is very important; describe how you will take better care of yourself?

- How will you surround yourself with positive sounds, thoughts and people?

- What specific negative influences need to be changed?

- What are your addictions and obsessive behaviors?

- What are new behaviors that you can put in their place?

- What self-talk needs to be replaced? List your new self-talk statements or affirmations.

- What expectations do you have of yourself? Are they realistic?

- Describe the expectations you have of others. Are they meeting your expectations? If not, how would you like them to be?

- Describe your destructive behaviors and how you can make better choices.

- Share one behavior with the group you want them to hold you accountable to each week. *Examples: work on the book you always wanted to write, get in shape, get organized, and do not procrastinate.*

Continued on next page

Chapter 6: Your Behaviors, Set Boundaries, Continued

Practice saying No

It takes practice to say No, when we have been so accustomed to saying Yes. Using the script you created earlier for ideas, practice what you would say to set healthy boundaries. Use the following pages for additional scripts you need to create and practice.

Perseverance

It takes works to establish boundaries. Recognize the behaviors in you that keep you from setting healthy boundaries now. Identifying those behaviors will help you transform into a women who can, "Walk through the front door, state what you want, and negotiate the difference." You can do it!

Notes:

Chapter 7: Inner Music

Purpose

The purpose of this Chapter is to help you start to "hear" your own inner music. Often inner music is a combination of negative self-talk, regrets and resentments. These thoughts are automatic and play repeatedly. They go unnoticed because they often begin in childhood. By beginning to articulate what you think and speak into your own life each day, you recognize this ultimately impacts your self-belief. By consciously beginning to change your thoughts you begin to carve new pathways of self-belief and self-talk.

"Are you a coffee addict?"

You desire it, can't imagine starting a day without it. You crave it, and your head hurts if you don't have it. As you wait in line for your delicious cup of java you realize that you are addicted. You are addicted to the "ups" and "downs" of caffeine.

While you wait in the coffee shop ordering line, music plays gently in the background, your toe taps and you may even sing the tune. When you exit the building with your coffee in hand, if asked what song was playing, you probably wouldn't remember. The music subconsciously registered and caused your mind to hear, and your body to react. The music could even have altered your mood without you consciously registering its effect on your beliefs, behaviors and moods.

Subconscious messages

Like the coffee story, there is background music playing in your head causing unconscious reactions.

The tune playing over and over in your head telling you what you can or cannot do, how lovable you are, and how good you are. The subconscious messages that you hear each day and each night can radically affect your mood, your self-esteem, your abilities and potential. Your inner music is your self-talk.

Continued on next page

Chapter 7: Inner Music, Continued

Your self-talk

It is hard to say when self-talk begins and what makes it degrade. When you observe a three-year old girl, often you see a confident princess who loves herself completely. When you watch a five-year old girl you may already detect limits, embarrassments or boundaries that she places on her abilities. What makes her self-esteem deteriorate in that short span of time?

When you are a woman at 13, 33, or 63, can you dance and sing and love yourself completely? You should! Unfortunately, you have spent so many years beating yourself up for all the qualities you lack, you live without loving yourself wholly or completely.

Plant Your Garden and Let it Grow

Let's pretend that you:

1. Plant the seedlings and wait for them to grow.
2. Give the seedlings dirty, toxic water.
3. Provide sporadic sunlight.
4. Get frustrated when only a few seedlings grow.

You eagerly await the growth of the new seedlings, despite the fact you have provided only doses of toxic water and sporadic sunlight. Your crop will be very thin and unproductive and they choke from lack of nourishment.

Would you ever do that? Not likely. You would love the seedlings making sure they had clean water and enough sunlight to survive. Without the proper nutrients, seedlings will not flourish and grow.

Realize that the seedlings are a metaphor of You.

You must fill your soul with daily doses of clean fresh water and pure sunlight so that you can grow healthy! Fill your spirit with daily doses of clean and healthy enrichments, not toxic nutrients.

How do you do that? You must fill your soul with clean and healthy, self-talk. Positive self-talk can make immediate changes. Take small strides, work at it and you will see a positive result.

Continued on next page

Chapter 7: Inner Music, Continued

Common self-talk	What does your inner music play?

Have you ever said:

- I am so fat. I'll never lose weight.

- I am so dumb. Why did I say that?

- I am so stupid.

- Why won't he just be nice to me?

- I feel so empty.

- No one knows how much I hurt inside.

- I hate my body.

- My family is so dysfunctional.

- I'll never get it right.

- No one loves me.

- People just don't know how hard I try.

- If I could just do better, I could get a handle on things.

- I am worthless.

- I messed up again. What's wrong with me?

- Don't they see how lonely I am inside?

- Why can't I just run away from here?

- I can't take any more pain.

- I must be crazy.

Continued on next page

Chapter 7: Inner Music, Continued

Your inner music

Often this self talk is Negative Automatic Talk that began as early as childhood.

What does your inner music play?

-
-
-
-
-

What people or events are occurring around when you think good thoughts?

What about negative thoughts?

Continued on next page

Chapter 7: Inner Music, Continued

What God wants you to know	**10 Things God wants you to remember:** 1. I am for you. 2. I love you. 3. I believe in you. 4. I will bless you. 5. I will give you rest. 6. I will be with you. 7. I will not fail you. 8. I will provide for you. 9. I will strengthen you. 10. I will answer you.

What should your music say?

Self-talk can be so destructive if allowed to play on repeat without intervention. Consciously decide what you want your music to say. You can change your music.

Listen to these encouraging statements of self-love:

- You are a perfect child of God and are beautiful in every way.
- You are perfect just the way you are.
- You were made unique with a special tool set that no one else in this world has.
- You are gorgeous, funny, smart, terrific, delectable, and scrumptiously unique.

"Set your mind on things above, not on things on the earth."

— Colossians 3:2 (NKJV)

Continued on next page

Chapter 7: Inner Music, Continued

Change your inner music

List **all** of the things that your inner music plays. Be descriptive and specific:

	REGRETS/RESENTMENTS		NEW
I always …		I always…	
I never …		I now…	
I wish …		I wish…	
Too bad I …		I am happy…	
If only I …		I love to…	

Continued on next page

Chapter 7: Inner Music, Continued

Acceptance

Learn to accept yourselves as God has made you. You are unique and marvelously made. Enjoy your uniqueness, enjoy the fact you have your "quirks," that is what makes you special.

"Thank you for making me so wonderfully complex! Your workmanship is marvelous - and how well I know it."

— Psalms 139:14 (NLT)

Affirmations

Affirmations are positive statements that we say or review often to change how we view ourselves. It can build self-esteem and support changing our self-talk. Self-talk and affirmations go hand in hand. Affirmations are one action to take to change your self-talk.

Consider these tips:

1. Affirmations should be written or in an audio or video recording. You can use your mobile phone and have your affirmations accessible anytime.
2. If written carry a copy in your wallet and every time you open your wallet read it silently or aloud.
3. Carry the affirmation in your car clipped to your visor. Each time you flip down the visor, read it aloud.
4. If possible, slide the piece of paper behind a light switch in a bathroom, bedroom, or kitchen and each time you enter and exit each room, you can say the affirmation aloud.
5. Write the affirmation five times every day on separate sheets of paper or in your journal.
6. Pray for God to reveal areas in your life that need to be transformed.

The key is to read it, say it, and write it. Repeat often.

Over time the affirmations reinforce and re-program the music inside our minds. When you feel that you can shout the affirmation and really believe it is true; pick a new affirmation. Repeat this process for the rest of your life.

Continued on next page

Chapter 7: Inner Music, Continued

Write your own affirmations

Sample affirmations:

- I am beautiful just as I am.

- I can do anything I set my mind to. I have all the tools and all the wisdom to be everything I can be.

- God has made me perfect and I love myself just as I am.

- I am a source of divine love and beauty.

- I trust my judgment and make good choices.

- I love myself and am able to clearly communicate boundaries with my family and friends in a loving and respectful manner.

Now write your own affirmations:

-

-

-

Continued on next page

Chapter 7: Inner Music, Continued

Limitless

The only limits you set are your own.

When you trust in spiritual wisdom and learn to accept that you are a beautiful creation of God, you grow. When you can walk by faith, rather than be driven by worries and fears, your life transforms. Set your goals, commit to staying the course, and you will see a new outcome.

"But Jesus looked at them and said, 'With men it is impossible, but not with God; for with God all things are possible.'"

— Mark 10:27 (NKJV)

Sorry cup

When you have experienced years of abuse, you find yourself always trying to appease or make others feel better. This tendency becomes a habit that you do not recognize that your speech pattern conveys a subservient message. One of the most overused words in our language is, "sorry."

Many unconsciously say the word "sorry" numerous times in a day to loved ones, coworkers and complete strangers. "Sorry" should be reserved to convey true sorrow for the injury or hurt inflicted on another person.

Overuse of this phrase puts you in a subservient position by accepting blame for items not your fault. Stop saying the word "sorry" unless you are conveying true sorrow for hurt you have caused to someone else.

Select a coffee mug and this is your new "Sorry" Cup. Every time you say the word, "sorry" put a quarter into the cup. If you follow this exercise in about one week you will break this habit.

You probably do not realize how often you say that 5-letter word. You can say, "I apologize," "oops," "excuse me," "I'll be done in a minute," "it's yours now," "yes, I made a mistake on that report," "yes, I missed that deadline," "no, I can't do that for you tonight."

Let's say you are at the copy machine at work, someone approaches you and says, "I need the machine." Instead of "I'm sorry," Instead try this, "Okay, I'll be done in a minute." That is all you have to say.

Try it and have fun spending your "sorry" money.

Notes:

Chapter 8: Parent-Child Hooks, Medical Impact

Purpose   Chapter 8 has two very important concepts.

First, to help you identify how you are "hooked" in conversations by what is said to you and how you automatically react and respond. Knowing these patterns exist, you can begin to change your reactions and responses.

Secondly, you need to be self-aware that you may have medical impacts and residual emotions from the difficulties you have endured in your life. Accepting and embracing the fact you are a woman. God created you with a woman's body and you have woman's issues, accepting those with self-love rather than self-hatred is important to healing inside and outside.

Continued on next page

Chapter 8: Parent-Child Hooks, Medical Impact, Continued

**Ego states
Parent, Adult,
Child**

A well-known and widely used theory still today states that all persons have three dimensions, or "ego states," the Parent, Adult, Child (PAC). This theory is a part of Transactional Analysis, the study of social intercourse, personality, relationships and social intercourse. Transactional Analysis (TA) was developed by Eric Berne and gained popularity when his book, *Games People Play,* was published in 1964. His work is a foundation to many therapy methods designed including the use of TA. [5]

Each ego state performs specific functions. We move seamlessly between each of the ego states based on our current situation and the interactions occurring with others at that time.

A healthy person has a happy mixture of Parent, Child and Adult with the **Adult driving the behavior**.

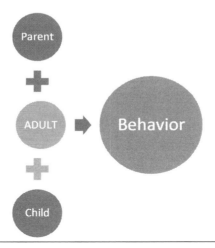

Figure 4. Adult Driving the Behavior.   Source: Stronger than Espresso, Inc. © 2014.

Trouble occurs when we get "hooked" by behavior from those around us and our Parent or Child behaviors take the lead. The Parent and Child states function actively through our lives in our behavior and relationships. [6]

Continued on next page

Chapter 8: Parent-Child Hooks, Medical Impact, Continued

Parent

The Parent ego state has two functions:

1. Giving us the ability to parent.

2. Automatic responses, "because that's the way it's done" or "because I said so." This state contains the attitudes, feelings and behavior patterns from our parents or authority figures.

There are two parts of the Parent ego:

1. Nurturing Parent —which is caring and loving.

2. Prejudicial Parent — full of demands, oughts and shoulds that you must follow. [7]

Adult

The adult ego state is necessary for survival and essential for coping with reality.

The adult state has these functions:

1. The state is logical and performs objective data processing.

2. A critical role for the Adult state is that it mediates the Parent and Child. [8]

3. The Adult is free to take information from the Parent and the Child and act in a constructive way.

4. The Adult that is autonomous and can function intentionally letting the Parent guide and let the Child play, when appropriate. [9]

Child

The childhood ego is fixed in early childhood and is activated in certain circumstances. The child state can be charming, creative, spontaneous, playful.

There are two parts to the Child ego state:

1. Adaptive Child —modifies behavior because of Parent and can be compliant or disobedient.

2. Natural and spontaneous — rebellion or creative. The Parent is the cause and the Child the effect.

Continued on next page

Chapter 8: Parent-Child Hooks, Medical Impact, Continued

Games defined

Berne's studies determined that "Games" are stereotyped, repetitive, mutually manipulative interactions between two people.

Games are defenses by which we seek to protect ourselves from not-okay feelings.

Every game has a pay-off for both people by perpetuating behaviors, feelings or fears that we believe to be true.

Games are the opposite of open, authentic, loving, and growing relationships. [10]

The beginning

Children observe their parents' games and adopt an unconscious life plan or "script," which they will use through their life. They determine an expectation, which causes them to behave so as to make their script come true.

To the degree that a person's games and scripts are functioning outside their awareness, they are locked into feelings and behavior programmed by their old Parent and Child tapes. In this circumstance, any feelings of autonomy or freedom are an illusion and their growth potential is frozen until the tapes are reprogrammed. [11]

Can adults change?

The Adult does have the power to change by empowering the inner Adult to change from programmed responses to more spontaneous, appropriate, and constructive responses in each situation.

As people become aware of their games and scripts, and the destructive consequences; the motivation to change increases. [12] Changing these scripts requires commitment, dedication and perseverance, but it can be done.

Continued on next page

Chapter 8: Parent-Child Hooks, Medical Impact, Continued

Equal states   As long as the interactions are complementary everything is smooth [13]:

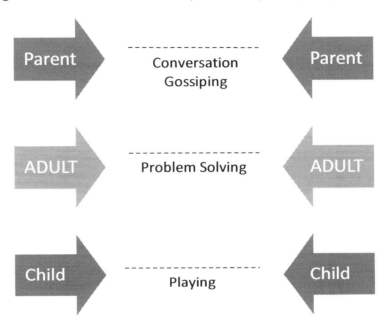

Figure 5. Complementary Behavior Interactions.   Source: Stronger than Espresso, Inc. © 2014.

Adult asks a question and receives a simple response from the other Adult. There is no emotion, no blame, no hidden agenda, just the answer to the question. When both individuals are in the parent or child states there is no problem.

Continued on next page

Chapter 8: Parent-Child Hooks, Medical Impact, Continued

Different states   Problems occur when these lines cross over.

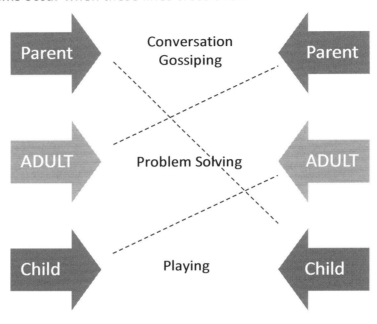

Figure 6. Behavior Interaction Crossover. Source: Stronger than Espresso, Inc. © 2014.

In the Parent and Child responses actions or words can translate into accusation, judgment, blame and criticism. This fuels emotion and is what it means to be "hooked."

Question in Adult Ego State	Response in Various Ego States
"Where are my keys?"	If Adult answers, *"On the desk."* If Parent answers, *"You are always losing things."* If Child answers, *"I hate it when you ask me to find your things.*
"Why are you drinking so much?"	If Adult answers, *"Yes I am. I hate my job right now."* If Parent answers, *"Why are you always criticizing me?"* If Child answers, *"Don't tell me what to do."*
"Is dinner ready?"	If Adult answers, *"Not yet."* If Parent answers, *"Why do I have to do everything?"* If Child answers, *"Quit blaming me."*

Continued on next page

Chapter 8: Parent-Child Hooks, Medical Impact, Continued

Back to adult state

You cannot return to the Adult state until the communication lines are cleared. This can take moments, days, months and years. In some cases couples are never able to return to the Adult state because of their games.

If you cannot remain in the Adult state, you will have the same discussion, fight, argument or interaction. This game will replay until you can adapt your behavior and response.

This communication folly perpetuates the games played between two people. To the extent that clear communication may be unable to exist outside this vicious cycle. [14]

You don't see them at first

These events are not random and have been programmed into your behavior over years of experience and practice.

The Adult and Parent roles are often displayed in new social settings and external environments. The Child behavior is shielded by the Adult and Parent until the waters have been tested. [15] Then it comes out.

That is often why after you have gotten to know someone, you start to see the real them. It is often their "child" that comes out and you see them react and interact in certain settings.

Break the cycle

So how do you break the cycle?

The games played go hand in hand with the coping behaviors learned earlier. They perpetuate the games. The most important thing that you can do is to be aware that you are being "hooked."

Once you identify the source, the scripts can be redesigned and rewritten to bring a new outcome.

Continued on next page

Chapter 8: Parent-Child Hooks, Medical Impact, Continued

Impact on relationships

The healthiest ego state is the Adult. Adults assume responsibility for their own behavior. Taking responsibility means that you do not blame others for your pain and suffering. You take control and do not release the ability for another to control your emotions.

Regardless of what ego state your partner demonstrates, you can choose which ego state you will respond with. Learn to ask God to help you respond. He will help you keep control. If they approach you as a child, you can respond from your adult state and stick to the facts. Problems can easily escalate when your Parent responds and reprimands their childish behavior.

Games are played in all relationships. When you are confronted with an argument, action or statement that "gets to you" how you react can make you play the game, or diffuse it. The next time that you are confronted with a situation that makes you uncomfortable, angry or sad, you have a choice on whether to let it "hook" you or not.

You will feel uncomfortable to do this at first. With God's help you will learn that he is in control and you can establish new pathways.

Impact with an abusive relationship

The challenge with an abusive relationship is that the same relationship rules do not always apply. Abusive cycles continue because the abuser blames others and there are complex emotional games that are played.

You believe that if you try hard enough, eventually they will be happy and stop hurting you. Once they are happy; you believe, you can finally achieve happiness too. If you continue to operate within the cycle of abuse and hope that the abuser will get better someday, you are fooling yourself.

Even if you remain in the Adult state it may not be enough to restore relationships with an abuser. Your good behavior will not change or improve this situation. You may have to distance yourself from the person or their behavior for complete healing. This could apply to a spouse, boyfriend, sister, brother, parent, coworker, or friend. Anyone who "hooks" you with inappropriate behavior and is abusive while you remain in the Adult state is not communicating in a healthy way.

You cannot change the abuser's behavior; you can only change your own.

Continued on next page

Chapter 8: Parent-Child Hooks, Medical Impact, Continued

Your response

Reflect on your answers in Chapter 4, Coping Mechanisms. The responses are a part of your hooks and perpetuate this game.

Start to recognize what your automatic responses are when someone "hooks" your emotional tender zones. It may take time to understand how you respond, but knowing how you react can help you begin to make changes.

You do not have to choose to play the same game. When you recognize game playing, stop and take a deep breath. Do not let it wound you to your inner core and hook the rebellious child. Instead try to put into perspective what is happening. Pray and ask God to give your guidance. You have the right to choose and decide what to do next.

It will take time, practice and prayer. You can do it. With God's help — you absolutely can do it! *"With God all things are possible."* — **Matthew 19:26**

Continued on next page

Chapter 8: Parent-Child Hooks, Medical Impact, Continued

List your hooks

Even if they do not reply in a healthy way — you do not have to be hooked!

List your top three items that "hook" you. Record what happens or what is said that has an impact. Describe what you normally feel and how you cope. Create your new response in the Adult state.

Performing this self-discovery will help you identify patterns and areas that "hook" you. The hook equals the same mood swing, emotional tail spin, or fight that you cannot seem to resolve or move beyond.

Here is an example:

Scenario: Husband never picks up his dirty clothes.

Emotions: You feel frustrated, used and disrespected.

Response: You grab all the clothes stuff them in the laundry basket. In response you spout off statements from either the Child or Parent ego state:

Child — "You are driving me crazy with this mess!"

Parent — "Why do I have to do everything?"

You could say, Adult — "Can you pick up your dirty clothes?"

Do not get "hooked" by your own feelings. You do not have to become a part of that emotional game. Recognize the destructive force it has on you and your ability to move out of the game playing role.

On the next page identify situations or statements that seem to "hook" you into trouble. Write how it makes you feel and create a response from your Adult ego state.

Continued on next page

Chapter 8: Parent-Child Hooks, Medical Impact, Continued

The Action or Statement	Your Emotion or Coping Behavior	Your New Adult Response
Example. Your kids make a mess all over the house and never clean up their toys.	*Pick up their toys, yell at them and slam them into a toy box so they know how upset you are.* *Or you pick toys up without saying a word but seething anger and stuff your frustration down deep.* *Or you cry and let them know how sad and hurt you are.*	*Require that they clean up their toys without you having any emotional response.*
1.		
2.		
3.		

Continued on next page

Chapter 8: Parent-Child Hooks, Medical Impact, Continued

You can reestablish a new parent

You carry an understanding of what a Parent should be based on the role models and your experiences growing up. As an adult you hold the hurts of your inner child and disappointments in the parenting you received. Let God's grace heal you:

- God is your perfect parent. Pure love. Pure grace.
- You can feel whole and receive all the wonderful qualities of the perfect parent.
- You can love your own child and heal from the hurts of the past.
- You can complete the void that is present.
- You have the power to love yourself through these times without looking for external reassurances.
- Your "hurts" of not being loved, fear of abandonment, or criticism received from your parents can be washed clean and no longer control your behavior.
- You can be free from your past.

"Behold what manner of love the Father has bestowed on us, that we should be called children of God."

— 1 John 3:1 (NKJV)

Over time

Over time you will be faced with another difficult situation and your "child" will run out in a rage and ready to have a temper tantrum. When this happens, pause for a moment and recall this visualization exercise. Let your Adult self come into the picture and hold the small child soothing their hurt. This validates your emotions and allows you to then face a problem without having an emotional "melt down."

> "The discovery of the inner child is really the discovery of a portal to the soul. The inner child keeps us human. It never grows up, it only becomes more sensitive and trusting as we learn how to give it the time, care and parenting it so richly deserves."

Source: From the book *Embracing Ourselves*. Copyright ©1989, by Hal Stone and Sidra Stone. Reprinted with permission of New World Library, Novato, CA. www.newworldlibrary.com.

Continued on next page

Chapter 8: Parent-Child Hooks, Medical Impact, Continued

**Reestablish a
New Parent**

Create a list of all the qualities of a Perfect Parent. There is no right answer and it will be unique and individual as you are.

- Write out the qualities your "Perfect Parent" would possess.

- All the qualities that you wish you had received from your parents.

- Qualities that you wish you had now with your children.

- What are ways you will reestablish this new parent into your life?

- How can you comfort your inner child when you struggle with an issue in the future?

Continued on next page

Chapter 8: Parent-Child Hooks, Medical Impact, Continued

New parent, next step

God is your ultimate Father. Even though we know how amazing it is that he knows us, we often feel discouraged because our own parent relationships left us feeling broken. In the last activity you established a new parent in your life. As an adult now, you have the ability to comfort yourself even if the wounds of childhood still hurt. Next, we will look at the medical impact abusive relationships can have on our life. Self-love is important, even if you feel weak, broken, or not good enough. God made you in His image and God loves you — just as you are. Broken, never looked so beautiful!

Why do I feel like this?

As any good coffee junkie knows…"Highs are high, lows are low, and without it, you crash." Your daily cup of coffee brings highs and if you don't get your daily dose, you can suffer some ill physical effects, such as: severe headache, confusion or irritability.

Our emotions are similar in that they vary from day-to-day and can be influenced by outside sources. However, you should be on the lookout for false highs and lows as they can be a sign of a serious medical condition.

In this lesson we will review common medical conditions that are the result of living in an abusive relationship. Just because they exist now does not mean they will remain for your lifetime. If you are experiencing these types of symptoms, it is not your fault.

Identifying them and getting the help you need is the key to your freedom.

Continued on next page

Chapter 8: Parent-Child Hooks, Medical Impact, Continued

Medical conditions

These are common medical issues that can occur for women that have been impacted by domestic abuse:

- Depression

- Addictive Behaviors

- Premenstrual Syndrome (PMS)

- Premenstrual Dysphonic Disorder (PMDD)

- Stockholm Syndrome

- Post-Traumatic Stress Disorder (PTSD)

- Chronic Anxiety

- Managing Trauma Symptoms

Continued on next page

Chapter 8: Parent-Child Hooks, Medical Impact, Continued

Depression

Depression impacts millions of people each day.

Depression is often defined as, "Extreme melancholy, often with a reduction in vitality and physical systems."[16] To have the blues from time to time is normal. When you experience these symptoms consistently for several weeks can be the first sign of depression. Situational depression, left untreated, can turn into chronic depression and before more serious.

Typically, emotional turmoil begins to affect your moods, sleep patterns, and eating habits, which over a period of time can accumulate into a substantial problem. When you are upset you lose sleep and do not eat right. Lack of sleep and improper diet can aggravate and worsen your mood. A downward cycle is created and intensifies depression.

Fortunately, it can be cured with either therapy, medication or a combination of the two. Depression can be very difficult to spot in yourself so understanding the symptoms can keep you vigilant in protecting your well-being.

Depression is **Anger Turned Inward.** [17]

You may not realize that you are angry, but through self-discovery you will locate the source of the emotions.

When you weed a garden, if you only pull the top leaves, the root remains. You have to dig deep to get to the cause. It can get your hands dirty to dig, but once you pull it out, the weed is gone!

Over time you stuff your anger down inside your innermost chambers pretending to be happy, and full of smiles for everyone to see. Yet this false front hides the fact you are emotionally hurting inside. You become immobilized to even cry out for help, and you hope that someone will notice your pain and sadness.

When you stuff feelings down, tension builds inside. At the foundation of your pain is ANGER. Anger is the emotion most closely aligned to your desire for self-preservation. What can be misleading is that anger can be, openly expressed, volatile and loud, or it can be silent and inward. Both forms of anger are equally as destructive. In any form, anger destroys the vessel it's in.

Continued on next page

Chapter 8: Parent-Child Hooks, Medical Impact, Continued

Are You Depressed?

Depression Inventory - Answer the questions with a Yes or No.

	Yes	No
1. Do you criticize yourself frequently?		
2. Do you think of yourself as weak, a failure, not good enough, unlovable, a loser, etc.?		
3. Do you feel irritated because of someone's imperfections or insensitivities?		
4. Do you sulk when you realize others don't agree with your views or preferences?		
5. Do you remain frustrated because of the unfair circumstances you encounter?		
6. Are you unable to feel compassion for yourself, or grant yourself forgiveness most of the time? Are you cruel to yourself when you make mistakes?		
7. Do you constantly fail to reach the standards set for yourself?		
8. Do you lack energy, and have trouble motivating yourself to do things? Do your arms, legs or back feel heavy, achy, and hard to move (not due to injury)?		
9. Do you promise to do a favor or help someone and then resent the fact that you have too much to do?		
10. Do you avoid people you need to confront?		
11. Do you speak in sharp tones?		
12. Do you have a short fuse? Then condemn yourself for having it?		
13. Are you described by others as moody or irritable?		
14. Do you feel hurt when a person fails to recognize your needs or perceptions?		
15. Do you hold resentments regarding others' insensitivities?		

Continued on next page

Chapter 8: Parent-Child Hooks, Medical Impact, Continued

	Yes	No
16. Do you feel agitated, restless, anxious much of the time?		
17. Do you believe that things are unlikely to get better?		
18. Do you think you are eating and sleeping way too much or way too little?		
19. Do you have regrets about the past that will not fade?		
20. Do you feel overwhelmed by your life?		
21. Do you feel emotionally numb?		
22. Are you frequently tearful; do you frequently feel sad for no apparent reason?		
23. Have you lost interest in activities you used to enjoy?		
24. Have you lost interest in sex?		
25. Are you having trouble concentrating, or making decisions?		
26. Do you find yourself continually trying to choose behavior to relieve you from your suffering? Such as eating, drinking alcohol, using drugs, having sex, putting yourself in danger, gambling, shopping, pornography or others.		
27. Are you withdrawing from people when you can?		
28. Do you wish for death to end your pain; do you think everyone would be better off if you were dead?		
29. Do you have any of the above experiences regularly with the cycle of your period? In the wintertime? Have you recently given birth?		
30. Do you worry excessively? Or are called pessimistic?		

Adapted from Source: National Alliance on Mental Illness (NAMI). *"About Mental Illness: Major Depression,"* NAMI.org. www.nami.org.

Continued on next page

Chapter 8: Parent-Child Hooks, Medical Impact, Continued

Scoring   If you answered "Yes" to two or more of these questions, you may be experiencing some form of depression. Pay close attention to the following questions because "if you catch yourself in one or more of the behaviors, you can be assured that anger is alive within your personality."

For more information visit National Alliance on Mental Illness (NAMI).

Get help   Don't be ashamed. Get the help you need.

Please get a professional evaluation by a medical doctor or seek therapy by a qualified counselor to relieve your suffering. If you need a referral, you can seek medical help and a doctor will refer you to a counselor. Counseling can really help. For more information about woman and depression check the National Association of Mental Illness, www.NAMI.org detailing depression.

You may also be eligible for free or low-cost counseling available for woman who have been abused. Contact the Stronger than Espresso® team to help, look for a Celebrate Recovery® program or resources through your church. Check your local phone book for hotline phone numbers for family centers or battered woman shelters, they can direct you to the resources that can help and are affordable.

Depression may not be the root cause; you may have signs of a different medical condition that can be identified with a simple exam or blood test.

If you ever feel in any danger of killing yourself or being killed, immediately call a local crisis line or visit www.suicidehotlines.com.[18]

"Women have to understand that regardless of who does not want us we have to want ourselves. Self-love is the first and hardest rule to stick by. Women need to not abandon themselves in their quest for bliss and love. You can love yourself spiritually, physically, in almost any way anybody else can."

Alice Walker, MS Magazine

Continued on next page

Chapter 8: Parent-Child Hooks, Medical Impact, Continued

Addictions

Addictive substances and compulsive behaviors directly affect our mental, physical and emotional health. Alcohol and drugs, over eat, inappropriate sexual behaviors, excessive use of money, coffee, food, exercise, smoking, shopping can develop into dangerous habits and hazardous to your health.

It is a vicious cycle:

- The more you use these behaviors as "Band-Aids" you avoid facing the issues that are the source of your pain.

- You numb yourself to your pain so that you can cope.

- The more pain you cover-up the more you need to mask your pain.

Recognize that every time you choose a dangerous behavior is one more time YOU choose and take responsibility for specific outcomes.

Continued on next page

Chapter 8: Parent-Child Hooks, Medical Impact, Continued

Evaluation of where you are emotionally

Now it is time to reflect on your emotions and conduct an emotional evaluation.

Answer the following questions to understand how you feel:

- How healthy do you want to live the rest of your life?

- Describe what would make you happier?

- Describe a time you recall being very happy.

- I can't help myself doing these addictive behaviors because ...

- The pain you are really trying to sooth is ...

- No one knows ...

- To get back at the one(s) who are hurting you ...

- The only way out is to ...

Continued on next page

Chapter 8: Parent-Child Hooks, Medical Impact, Continued

Secondary gain   Have you ever heard of the concept of secondary gain? Secondary gain is an external motivator that keeps us from moving ahead in one direction because it has a greater hold on us than what we say we really want.

Here's an example:

Participant *"I want to go to the gym but I am too tired after working each day."*

Instructor: *Why do you want to go to the gym?*

Participant Answer: *To be healthier, lose weight.*

Instructor: *When you get off work what keeps you from going?*

Participant Answer: *"Tired, etc..."*

Instructor: *"Class what solutions do you see for her?" Class responds, "She could go at a different time of day." "What do you think of that idea?"*

Participant Answer: *"Well, I really don't feel comfortable going?"*

Instructor: *"Tell me more about that."*

Participant Answer: *"There are too many people."*

Instructor: *"Why do too many people bother you?"*

Participant Answer: *"I am embarrassed about my body."*

Instructor: *"What do you feel when you are embarrassed?*

Participant Answer: *Fear, Unworthy, Ugly, etc...*

In this example her FEAR of being embarrassed and not being good enough was greater than her DESIRE to be healthy and lose weight. Only by dissecting this thought process could we identify what was really driving the decision. This is the concept of secondary gain.

Continued on next page

Chapter 8: Parent-Child Hooks, Medical Impact, Continued

Girl to Girl

Here are important points to consider:

- If you can't be sober with the man you are with and he can't be sober with you, then send him packing.

- If you have "self-destructive" behaviors, <u>do not</u> choose a partner who has the same habits. In time, you will succumb to those habits yourself and revert back to the person of your past, not the new self you are working to create and preserve.

- Respect yourself. Respect the body, the heart, the lungs, the liver, the cells, the skin, and the sexual organs that your maker gave you. You are special, one of a kind, and deserve to have the longest, richest life possible.

- Alcohol can worsen depression! If you think those drinks are "making you feel better," you are incorrect.

- When you are drinking, it is easy to begin to cloud your judgment and to feel there is no escape from your pain. Do not allow your thoughts to go down the suicidal path. Reach out to someone. Even though you may not believe it right now, there are so many alternatives to ease your pain. Don't miss divine light shining on you.

- If nothing else gets your attention, how about the fact that alcohol is full of calories! It can make your waist line thick and give you a tummy pooch. Quitting or severely cutting back can bring results within a few weeks - honest!

- Do not replace one behavior with another one. If you quit drinking, don't replace it with: compulsive eating, gambling, prescription drugs, illegal drugs or sex. Join a gym and let out your tension, take a dance classes or workout with a friend. Walk and walk and walk. Find healthy solutions to replace past behavior.

- Phone a friend! Don't be alone. That is when we are at our weakest time to make poor choices. Call and connect.

Continued on next page

Chapter 8: Parent-Child Hooks, Medical Impact, Continued

I NEED my coffee

You wait in line for your coffee, tapping your toes incessantly, agitated because you have had a very bad morning. It started with a full blown fashion crisis because every pair of pants didn't fit and your butt and thighs transformed into large cellulose stumps overnight. Grumbling under your breath, you know that everyone exists today just to upset you. "Non-fat latte with a double shot!" the barista yells. You step to the counter and a smiling face chirps, "Have a nice day." Snarling you grab your coffee and think, "If you don't wipe that smile off your face, I am going to make your day!" You leave the coffee shop feeling like a raging maniac. Your abdomen is cramping, it hurts to stand, your stomach is weak with nausea and you feel a migraine headache coming on. What are you experiencing? Yes, it is full blown PMS!

It's real not just in your head

Premenstrual Syndrome (PMS) and Premenstrual Dysphonic Disorder (PMDD) are very real conditions and must be embraced with love and understanding. If you remain at odds with your body and ignore your monthly cycles, it can be very damaging. Regardless of what jokes can be made, you need to understand that women, namely you, need self-love during this time. Some women may not be affected, others have mild symptoms, but many women become so affected that their daily lives are interrupted with their menses cycle. It is vital that you look at this monthly event as a part of your patterns of behavior. Like it or not, you must embrace your womanhood and understand times when you need to demand more self-love and love from others.

Definition: PMS

Premenstrual syndrome (PMS) is a group of symptoms related to the menstrual cycle. PMS symptoms occur in the week or two weeks before your period (menstruation or monthly bleeding). The symptoms usually go away after your period starts. PMS may interfere with your normal activities at home, school, or work. Menopause, when monthly periods stop, brings an end to PMS.

Continued on next page

Chapter 8: Parent-Child Hooks, Medical Impact, Continued

PMS Causes / Symptoms

The causes of PMS are not yet clear. Some women may be more sensitive than others to changing hormone levels during the menstrual cycle. Stress does not seem to cause PMS, but can make it worse. PMS can affect menstruating women of any age.

PMS often includes both physical and emotional symptoms. Diagnosis of PMS is usually based on your symptoms, when they occur, and how much they affect your life.

PMS often includes both physical and emotional symptoms. Common symptoms are:

- breast swelling and tenderness
- fatigue and trouble sleeping
- upset stomach, bloating, constipation or diarrhea
- headache
- appetite changes or food cravings
- joint or muscle pain
- tension, irritability, mood swings, or crying spells
- anxiety or depression
- trouble concentrating or remembering

Symptoms vary from one woman to another. If you think you have PMS, try keeping track of your symptoms for several menstrual cycles. You can use a calendar to note which symptoms you are having on which days of your cycle, and how bad the symptoms are. Keep a daily record of your cravings, food intake, irritability and physical symptoms. Then seek medical guidance from your local physician or an OB/GYN to discuss your symptoms and treatment options.

Estimates of the percentage of women affected by PMS vary widely. According to the American College of Obstetricians and Gynecologists, up to 40 percent of menstruating women report symptoms of PMS. Most of these women have symptoms that are fairly mild and do not need treatment. Some women (perhaps five to ten percent of menstruating women) have a more severe form of PMS. [19]

Continued on next page

Chapter 8: Parent-Child Hooks, Medical Impact, Continued

PMS Treatments

Many treatments have been tried for easing the symptoms of PMS. However, no treatment has been found that works for everyone. A combination of lifestyle changes and other treatment may be needed. [20] If your PMS is not debilitating, a healthier lifestyle may help you feel better and cope with symptoms.

- Neurotransmitters are produced in the brain from components of certain foods. A stable brain serotonin level is associated with a positive mood state. It appears that women have a greater sensitivity than men to changes in this brain chemical. Mood swings during the menstrual cycle and menopause are thought to be caused by hormonal changes that influence the production of serotonin. [21]

- How does diet play a role? The foods that increase the production of serotonin in the brain are high in carbohydrates. Many foods contain carbohydrates, such as candy, cereal, and pasta, can produce a temporary increase in brain serotonin—and a subsequent calming or anxiety-reducing effect. Carbohydrates affect brain serotonin because they increase the amount of tryptophan in the brain. Tryptophan is the amino-acid precursor of serotonin. Carbohydrate-rich foods influence serotonin level in the brain by boosting blood insulin. Insulin assists tryptophan transport across the blood brain barrier causing serotonin levels to rise. [22]

- Carbohydrate-rich meals (whole grain breads, crackers, rice, potato, pasta) often increase serotonin levels.

- Vegetables, fruit and beans are carbohydrates, but feed into your system slowly. A good rule is to eat four cups of brightly colored veggies a day.

- Candy, sweets and chocolate, are simple carbohydrates, which can increase serotonin levels, but the effect will only last 1 - 2 hours.

Continued on next page

Chapter 8: Parent-Child Hooks, Medical Impact, Continued

PMS Treatments (continued)

- pH Factor – Our bodies have a delicate pH balance. When our bodies run acidic it can cause a variety of health issues. Joint paint, anxiousness, sleeplessness and other disorders can be from the body being acidic. Coffee, soda, alcohol, refined sugars all strip the body of alkaline. Only fresh vegetables, fruits and whole grains can improve this condition.

- Check if you are low in Vitamin D or B12 which can lower energy levels, memory loss, confusion and other symptoms. Simple blood tests can check these levels and easily can be added to your daily vitamin regime.

- Protein, lean meats, dairy, and nuts can be eaten three times a day.

- Be sure that you are getting enough vitamins and minerals. Take a multivitamin every day that includes 400 micrograms of folic acid. A calcium supplement with vitamin D can help keep bones strong and may help with PMS symptoms.

- Adopt a healthier way of life. Exercise regularly, get enough sleep, choose healthy foods, don't smoke, and find ways to manage stress in your life.

- Try avoiding excess salt, sugary foods, caffeine, and alcohol, especially when you are having PMS symptoms.

- In more severe cases, drugs such as diuretics, ibuprofen, birth control pills, or antidepressants may be used.

- Although PMS does not seem to be related to abnormal hormone levels, some women respond to hormonal treatment. For example, one approach has been to use drugs such as birth control pills to stop ovulation from occurring. Antidepressants that alter serotonin in the body have been shown to help many women with severe PMS.

Continued on next page

Chapter 8: Parent-Child Hooks, Medical Impact, Continued

Premenstrual Dysphonic Disorder (PMDD)

Premenstrual Dysphonic Disorder (PMDD) is a severe, disabling form of PMS. In PMDD, the main symptoms are mood disorders such as depression, anxiety, tension, and persistent anger or irritability.

These severe symptoms lead to problems with relationships and carrying out normal activities. Women with PMDD usually also have physical symptoms, such as headache, joint and muscle pain, lack of energy, bloating and breast tenderness. According to the American Psychiatric Association, a woman must have at least five of the typical symptoms to be diagnosed with PMDD. The symptoms must occur during the two weeks before her period and go away when bleeding begins.

Research has shown that antidepressants can help many women with PMDD. [23]

By taking the initiative and understanding your cycle, you can identify special times when you need more self-love. You may not have the patience, and you may be more moody and prone to tears. Your sadness, hopelessness and discomfort could be another pattern on top of the daily abuse you endure.

For more information contact the Office on Women's Health in the Department of Health and Human Services or the National Women's Health Information Center at www.4woman.gov.

Continued on next page

Chapter 8: Parent-Child Hooks, Medical Impact, Continued

Stockholm Syndrome

It is common for people to criticize and say, "Why doesn't she just leave?"

Often victims of domestic abuse have an emotional bond with the abuser and this is identified as Stockholm Syndrome. It can be found in family, romantic and interpersonal relationships, and is a strategy victims' of abuse use for survival. Once you accept the impact that this bonding can have, you can begin to understand the behavior and why many stay.

The Stockholm Syndrome is named after an event on August 23, 1978 where two criminals carrying machine guns entered a bank in Stockholm, Sweden. They took four hostages, strapped them with dynamite and held them for 131 hours. After the rescue, despite the fact they feared for their lives, they supported the captors and began to feel the captors were protecting them from the police.

When certain conditions exist, the Syndrome can cripple the victim's ability to operate autonomously and see the situation clearly.

1. The abused victim perceives a threat to their survival and believes that the abuser will carry this out.
2. The victim will often perceive some form of kindness from the abuser. The victim is often isolated from others, or given incorrect information about the situation.
3. Believe they are unable to escape the situation.
4. Victims will often support, love and defend their abusers even when it does not appear logical to others. [24]

Understanding that you may be affected by this Syndrome, may allow you to work through breaking away. Recognize that your love and loyalty is not something you have done wrong or should be ashamed of. Discuss this with your therapist or counselor so they can assist you in recovery.

Continued on next page

Chapter 8: Parent-Child Hooks, Medical Impact, Continued

Post-Traumatic Stress Disorder (PTSD)

Everyday life contains stress and there are many ways you can choose to deal with it. Post-Traumatic Stress Disorder (PTSD) is a result of extreme stress and trauma and can be caused by a personal tragedy, accident, war, abuse or violent occurrence. PTSD is diagnosed when trauma escalates the normal reactions to stress into a "super-stress."

Despite your best efforts of good stress management, you are still overwhelmed. When you feel threatened by this stress, the terror and horror can be so overwhelming that you lose memory and may even faint. Victims of sexual or physical abuse or an assault may have these symptoms. The world as you knew it has been changed. It no longer is safe, people cannot be trusted, your self-esteem is destroyed; faith and hope are lost. This reaction to stress can remain with you for days, weeks, years or a lifetime. [25]

It is recommended that if you have experienced severe trauma you should seek medical help. If you are feeling overwhelmed, it is not because you are crazy or weak, but because you are affected by a medical condition.

Seeking group or individual therapy selecting a healthy lifestyle, and practicing relaxation techniques are all positive ways to begin. Unhealthy ways to deal with this stress include alcohol or drugs, running from the situation, or confronting the situation without the proper assistance.

Recognizing that you are having this problem is your first step. There are many resources available to assist you. For more information begin with your counselor or review information at the National Center for PTSD. www.ncptsd.va.gov.

"The Human Spirit is virtually indestructible and its ability to rise from the ashes remains as long as the body draws breath!" [26]

Author, Unknown

Continued on next page

Chapter 8: Parent-Child Hooks, Medical Impact, Continued

Managing Trauma Symptoms

How do I fix these issues?

When traumatic events happen it may be months or years before you are able to get over what occurred. These events can leave long lasting symptoms of anxiety, depression, fear, flashbacks, nightmares, and phobias. Sometimes the symptoms of the trauma can also be diagnosed as a psychiatric or mental illness such as depression, bipolar, schizophrenia, and other disorders.

Your treatment plan will be based on the breadth of your impact and whether or not your symptoms originate from a medical condition or from your trauma. [27]

To be restored ask God to shine His light on your next right step. Learning to trust his guidance will help you receive his blessings. Dedicate to working the Stronger than Espresso® program, connect with other woman and break the patterns of your past.

Continued on next page

Chapter 8: Parent-Child Hooks, Medical Impact, Continued

Trauma medical impact

Do you experience any of the following?

✔	Symptom
	Agitation
	Anxiety
	Cannot concentrate
	Chest pains or discomfort
	Chills or hot flashes
	Compulsive behaviors
	Detached from self
	Disconnected to world
	Dizziness or lightheaded
	Eating problems
	Emotionally "shut down"
	Fear of losing control or going crazy
	Feeling of impending doom / fear of dying
	Flashbacks
	Insomnia
	Irritability or rage
	Muscle tension
	Nausea, diarrhea, constipation, cramping
	Numbness
	Palpitations, fast heart rate, pounding heart
	Shaking or trembling
	Shortness of breath
	Terrified
	Unreality, confused about reality of the truth

Trauma scoring

If you checked "Yes" to more than two of these items, you are most likely dealing with trauma symptoms, or you may have a serious medical condition that needs attention.[28]

Seek the help of a physician and/or therapist to discuss how to manage these symptoms. Be comforted that in time they will pass and that you have the ability to heal 100%. The memories may never leave you, but the power and control they have over your emotional well-being will.

Continued on next page

Chapter 8: Parent-Child Hooks, Medical Impact, Continued

New ways to handle trauma

Right now you are responding with automatic reactions that you created in unhealthy settings and need to be reprogrammed. Your conscious mind <u>can</u> install new ways of handling situations by practicing a new response.

1. Review all of your "Yes" answers to the previous Trauma Medical Impact Evaluation and list them in the left column of this table.

2. Write out how you will handle the trauma when it occurs.

"Yes" item(s) from Trauma Medical Impact Activity	New Methods to Handle
Agitation. My rage and irritability is from not being able to control others.	*When I feel Agitation, I will take a deep breath and count to 10 slowly. I will be aware of my body responding, jaw clenching, fists forming, heart pounding and practice the principles of A-B-C. I will relax. I will reassure myself that I am okay right now and can handle anything that comes my way.*

Continued on next page

Chapter 8: Parent-Child Hooks, Medical Impact, Continued

New ways to handle trauma (continued)

"Yes" item(s) from Trauma Medical Impact Activity	New Methods to Handle

Continued on next page

Chapter 8: Parent-Child Hooks, Medical Impact, Continued

Chronic anxiety

Living with chronic anxiety and tension is exhausting. Intensive attempts to people please, strive for perfectionism, and components of fear create cycling patterns of lack of control in our own lives and in our relationships. Despite your circumstances by identifying today your own behavior and making a few changes, you will be able to reduce chronic anxiety and tension.

Anxiety evaluation

Answer the following questions to understand how you may be impacted by chronic anxiety:

Question	YES /NO
1. Do you feel an intense need for approval from others?	
2. Do you have an intense need for control?	
3. Are you uncomfortable letting others be in charge of a situation?	
4. Do you believe that if you are not in control, that you are weak and a failure?	
5. Do you tend to be a perfectionist and self-critical?	
6. Do you feel that what you do is never enough or not good enough?	
7. Do you often criticize your own efforts and feel a constant pressure to achieve?	

Continued on next page

Chapter 8: Parent-Child Hooks, Medical Impact, Continued

Anxiety evaluation (continued)

Review the answers defined:

- **Question 1.** If yes, you are a people pleaser. You typically put the needs of others before your needs, and this can lead to intense feelings of frustration and, over time, build resentment.

  People pleasing should have limits and not subject you to play the martyr. Often you know no other way and cannot imagine life in your home if you didn't "do what you do." If you feel haggard, jumpy, exhausted, or nervous, you may be seeking approval from others and denying your own needs. This denial can contribute to chronic anxiety and tension. This is also a symptom of codependent behavior.

- **Questions 2–4.** If yes, then you are being swallowed by your need for control. Your desire to be in-control situations comes from your feeling emotionally "out of control." You try to control the things you can with an unhealthy balance. This overwhelming need can lead to chronic stress, anxiety and even panic behaviors.

- **Questions 5–7.** If yes, you have a need to be perfect. No one is perfect. Your need to be perfect stems from your intense need for approval and your need for control (answered to Questions 1 and 2 above). You believe you can satisfy — if you are perfect. Self-criticism only leads to chronic anxiety and stress.

Source: Adapted from Women in Distress of Broward County, Inc., *Managing Anxiety*, Women In Distress of Broward County, Inc.[29]

Don't be anxious

We have God's word concerning anxiousness —don't do it!

What a promise! The peace of God. How comforting, how easy would it be to lean into his chest and listen to his heartbeat?

"Be anxious for nothing, but in everything by prayer and supplication, with thanksgiving, let your request be made known to God; and the peace of God, which surpasses all understanding, will guard your hearts and minds through Christ Jesus."

— Philippians 4:6,7 (NKJV)

Continued on next page

Chapter 8: Parent-Child Hooks, Medical Impact, Continued

What to Do When Symptoms Happen?

When the anxiety begins, your heart pounds, your hands clam up and you frantically look for the exits. Here are three medicine-free ways to try to calm and soothe yourself.

1. Pray. There are numerous scriptures that help us know to not be anxious and do not be afraid, just be still.

   Studying certain scriptures is a good place to begin.

   Review **Psalms 46:10, Exodus 14:14, and Philippians 4:6-7**.

2. Practice Principles of A B C [30]

   A. Acceptance of Self and what is happening.

      Awareness of Surroundings and Safety.

   B. Breathe.

   C. Concentrate and Choose to Change.

      Negative Thoughts to Positive Thoughts.

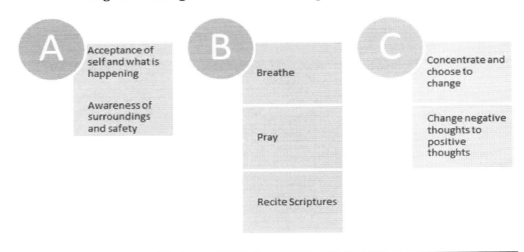

Figure 7. Handling Anxiety Symptoms.   Source: Stronger than Espresso, Inc. © 2014.

3. Phone a friend, coach, mentor, counselor, sponsor, accountability partner, neighbor, or coworker. Don't be alone; reach out for help and support.

Continued on next page

Chapter 8: Parent-Child Hooks, Medical Impact, Continued

Seek help

Review your answers to the questions on chronic anxiety or stress.

It is advised that during this time you seek the help of Christian women in the church, women Pastors, or Pastor's wives.

You can move beyond the chronic phase, but it may require a treatment plan. Should you, at any time, feel that you cannot go on or are in danger of hurting yourself, contact someone immediately.

Your soul is a blessing to our earth and must be allowed to blossom, live and experience the life that it has been gifted.

Section Two Summary

In review

Embracing your patterns of behavior is critical to begin your recovery. You must know each of your pieces so you can complete your own puzzle. Once you have honestly identified patterns, you can make conscious changes to your behavior. These changes can be implemented and change your life.

Actions

Begin changing your life:

- Reoccurring themes. Go back and review the Q & A or your notes for any "hot spots" or areas that really speak to you. Journal out your feelings as to why they touch you to be clear in your mind why you continue to choose that behavior.

    - Practice setting boundaries.

    - You have the right to say "No", be happy and be loved.

    - Self talk – what does your music say?

        o How will you plant and care for your garden?

        o Affirmations.

    - What are your Parent-child hooks?

    - Did you identify and evaluate your relationship patterns?

    - Are you depressed?

    - How are you managing addictive behavior?

    - How are you affected by the medical impact of abuse?

My VIPs

What were the most Valuable Important Points (VIPs) you learned in this Section:

-

-

-

Continued on next page

Section Two Summary, Continued

Study   Scripture review of the Section. Use this list for further personal study to understand God's word:

Scripture	Objective	Personal Thoughts
Ecclesiastes 3:1–8	Self-esteem – Confidence	
Matthew 7:7–8	Self-esteem	
Proverbs 21:23	Forgiveness – Grow beyond	
Matthew 11:28–30	Spirituality – Love Knowledge – Wisdom	
1 Peter 5:6–7	Self-esteem – Confidence	
Psalms 9:10	Self-esteem – Confidence	
1 Chronicles 7:14	Spiritual – Love	
Colossians 3:2	Connections Knowledge – Wisdom	
Psalms 119:133	Forgiveness – Grow beyond	
Philippians 4:6–7	Self-esteem – Confidence	
Romans 10:9	Spirituality – Love Self-esteem – Confidence	
Psalms 139:14	Self-esteem – Confidence	
Mark 10:27	Self-esteem – Achievement	
1 John 3:1	Spirituality – Love	
Psalms 46:10	Self-esteem – Confidence	
Exodus 14:14	Self-esteem – Confidence	

Section 3: Understanding Abusive Relationships

Overview

Introduction

The next step to the recovery process is to identify how you got here. This Section helps you clearly understand what behavior is abusive and how to recognize the warning signs to protect yourself now, and in future relationships.

Contents

This section contains the following topics:

Topic	See Page
Chapter 9: Powerless, Forgiveness, Bitterness	155
Chapter 10: Types of Abuse, Cycles, Safety, Legal	173
Section Three Summary	211

Objectives

Upon completion of this Section, you will be able to:

- Describe the status of current relationships.
- Demonstrate the ability to assess levels of danger.
- Develop methods to overcome bitterness and forgiveness.
- Identify types of abuse.
- Define cycle of violence.

Notes:

Chapter 9: Powerless, Forgiveness, Bitterness

Purpose

The purpose of Chapter 9 is for you to recognize that even though abuse in your life left a residual impact you are no longer powerless to your past. You CAN forgive and remove bitterness from your heart. By releasing these toxic emotions and burdens from the past you can become independent of your past and let God move more freely in your life.

Change

You cannot change the abuser, but you can change yourself. Arm yourself with knowledge so you can understand what you can change, and what you cannot. You do not have to repeat the past but in order to grow beyond it you must face the truth and learn from it.

"...His own special people, that you may proclaim the praises of Him who called you out of darkness into His marvelous light."

— 1 Peter 2:9 (NKJV)

The Fence:

There was a little boy with a bad temper. His father gave him a bag of nails and told him to hammer a nail in the back fence every time he lost control of his temper. The first day the boy drove 37 nails into the fence. Then it gradually dwindled down. He discovered that it was easier to hold his temper than to drive those nails into the fence. Finally the day came when the boy didn't lose his temper at all.

His father suggested that the boy now pull out one nail for each day that he was able to hold his temper. The days passed and the young boy was finally able to tell his father that all the nails were gone.

The father led his son to the fence. "You have done well, but look at the holes in the fence," he said, "When you say things in anger, they leave a scar just like these nail holes. You can put a knife in a person and draw it out. It won't matter how many times you say, I am sorry. The wound is still there. A verbal wound is as bad as a physical one." [31]

Author Unknown

Continued on next page

Chapter 9: Powerless, Forgiveness, Bitterness, Continued

I was embarrassed

"My pattern of abusive relationships was kept hidden because I was an educated, smart woman, too ashamed to let everyone know how awful it was. I was always gullible or captivated by their promises and "grass is greener story"— and every time I would fall in love with the wrong kind of man. After it occurred so many times, I was embarrassed to admit my mistake to myself, family or friends. I felt alone and unable to share my true feelings with anyone I could trust."

Identify Holes

Like the fencepost story, your "holes" will never disappear; however, you can mend your fence or even build a new one. God's love can fill those holes. Once you allow Him in you will find great joy and satisfaction in building your new life.

God promises you will be washed, *"...white as snow."*

— Isaiah 1:18 (NIV), Psalms 51:7 (NIV)

Right now you are a combination of the many experiences you have gathered to this point and hopes of who you wish to become. You cannot erase your past, but you must learn to embrace it with love. Admit that the holes exist and learn to love the character and uniqueness that they provide you. No one has the same experience or pattern; yours is custom made. That makes you unique and one of a kind.

Like the fencepost, you can have scars left from the verbal, emotional or physical "hits" from the past. Describe your holes and scars from the past. Identify events or people that make your heart feel sad, mad, glad or scared.

Continued on next page

Chapter 9: Powerless, Forgiveness, Bitterness, Continued

Memory Lane

Take time to reflect and record memories by age to celebrate the good memories and evaluate any negative experiences. Doing this can help you identify patterns and create any solutions to overcome negative emotions you may still have.

Record all the memories you can recall in specific age categories. Make sure to include good and bad memories.

Under age 5	
Age 5-10	
Age 11-15	
Age 16-20	

Continued on next page

Chapter 9: Powerless, Forgiveness, Bitterness, Continued

Age 21-30	
Age 31-40	
Age 41-50	
Age 51-60	
Age 61-70	
Age 71+	

Continued on next page

Chapter 9: Powerless, Forgiveness, Bitterness, Continued

Common themes:	Review your memories for common people, places, events, situations. Record those similarities here: <ul><li></li><li></li><li></li><li></li><li></li><li></li><li></li></ul>
New ideas to overcome	Brainstorm ideas to release your past: <ul><li></li><li></li><li></li><li></li><li></li><li></li><li></li><li></li><li></li></ul>

Chapter 9: Powerless, Forgiveness, Bitterness, Continued

God never waste a hurt	Your experiences matter to God. He never wastes a hurt. *"³ Blessed be the God and Father of our Lord Jesus Christ, the Father of mercies and God of all comfort, ⁴ who comforts us in all our tribulation, that [she] may be able to comfort those who are in any trouble, with the comfort with which [she is] comforted by God."* **— 2 Corinthians 1:3–4 (NKJV)**
The right question to ask	"Why Do You Stay?" A continuous question that so many of us have and we struggle as we watch women we love battle this problem. Stay for fear, stay for love, stay to avoid shame. Helping women see that their sense of normal has shifted can help them explain why they do what they do. The real question we should be asking is, "Why they abuse?"
No one understood	*Many people said to my face, "Why do you stay with him if it's so bad? Why don't you just leave?" Behind my back I would hear people saying, "Well, if it's really that bad, she should leave That doesn't make sense. She's asking for it if she just stays. We can't really help her, if she won't help herself."*

Continued on next page

Chapter 9: Powerless, Forgiveness, Bitterness, Continued

Why Do You Stay?

The answer to these questions can be understood if you study the long lasting emotional damage done to victims of domestic abuse. Earlier we learned the medical impacts abuse can have. The Stockholm Syndrome clearly demonstrates one example of how victims can shift in their normalcy. This Syndrome can be found in any relationship within a family, friendship, professional or romantic setting.

The abuser's role is one of control or authority, such as a parent, spouse or partner, or boss. The victims' strategy to survive the abuse is to emotionally bond with the abuser. The victim supports, loves and even defends their abuser because of the emotional bonding that occurs.

Emotional bonding occurs when all four conditions are to be true:

1. Perceived threat to one's survival and they believe the threat is real.
2. Perceived small acts of kindness from the abuser.
3. Isolation from the perspectives of others or from information about the situation.
4. Perceived inability to escape the situation. [32]

Abuser traits

An abuser will not "show all their traits" at the beginning. Rather they will reel in the victim, test them and ensure that they will be able to be controlled. The abuser may or may not be consciously aware that they are "reeling" you in. Many times, they have emotional or mental problems, or are a product of family heritage that has taught them how to treat others, which gives them a justification in their mind that this behavior is acceptable. Over time the victim becomes accustomed to certain behaviors and expected responses.

Continued on next page

Chapter 9: Powerless, Forgiveness, Bitterness, Continued

Normalcy Shifts   When you are subjected to abuse day after day your tolerance level increases and your basis of normalcy begins to shift. This shift alters your view of what is acceptable behavior and you become able to withstand further abuse.

Remember Figure 3. *When "Normal" Shifts* from Chapter 4?

The abuse increases gradually. You would likely head for the exit door if you were subject to a higher level of abuse immediately.

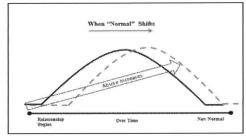

As normal shifts the following occurs:

- You receive a small amount of praise from the abuser and gain hope that this situation will improve.

- Your self-esteem is damaged. You begin to believe you are the cause of the trouble. Falsely thinking you can improve your treatment by acting "good."

- Often you are isolated from your friends, coworkers, neighbors, and family members so the true reality of your situation is not apparent to them. The isolation makes your world smaller and smaller, and often the only link to the outside world is your abuser.

- Often the abuser's demands and emotional ups and downs require enormous amounts of energy and time. Their behavior drains your energy level to exhaustion levels.

- The volatile nature and fear of the abuser requires you to sleep with one eye open. Sleep deprivation starts to play tricks on you. You become sleep deprived because you live in fear. Over time this distorts the truth and leaves you less able to differentiate your current situation from a healthy reality.

- Without the ability to set boundaries and stop the cycle, the chances you will run away continue to decrease. Even though your heart and body wisdom scream that this situation is not good for you, you are held emotionally captive.

Continued on next page

Chapter 9: Powerless, Forgiveness, Bitterness, Continued

Normalcy Shifts
(continued)

- You grow too numb to discern and decode your feelings.

- You may not be physically confined, capture or kidnapped, but you are mentally conditioned to believe there is no ability to escape. In your mind leaving the situation is not an option.

- Even if you do "get away" they create so much drama in your life you still can't get free. They hound you to get back together, threaten to take you to court, play cat and mouse games using the children as bait, harass you with repeated contact or stalk you in your movements.

In what ways has your "normal" shifted?

Describe people or situations that make you feel this way?

What are ways you can keep this from happening again?

Continued on next page

Chapter 9: Powerless, Forgiveness, Bitterness, Continued

Powerless

Many of us grew up powerless. Powerless perpetuates our victim mentality. When we are child, we reasoned like a child. As we mature we need to put those ways behind us and gain power over our decisions, our lives, and our future.

Has anyone ever done anything in your childhood that left you feeling powerless?

*"¹¹ When I was a child, I talked like a child, I thought like a child, I reasoned like a child. **[Your sense of being Powerless]** When I became a man, I put the ways of childhood behind me. **[Victory over Victim Mentality]** ¹² For now we see only a reflection as in a mirror; then we shall see face to face. Now I know in part; then I shall know fully, even as I am fully known."*
— 1 Corinthians 13:11, 12 (NIV)

Biblical View on Violence

What does the Bible say regarding family violence:

"Give up your violence and oppression and do what is right."
— Ezekiel 45:9 (NIV)

"Do not make friends with a hot tempered man, do not associate with one easily angered."
— Proverbs 22:24 (NIV)

"A hot-tempered man must pay the penalty if you rescue him, you will have to do it again."
— Proverbs 19:19 (NIV)

Continued on next page

Chapter 9: Powerless, Forgiveness, Bitterness, Continued

Coffee	Be prepared to sip on the strong, bitter drink until you are pumped up with the energy you need. Come on girls, drink it up and jolt awake!
Explore and let go, for good	If you do not fully explore your patterns of behavior, you will find yourself back into another abusive relationship. Asking God to transform your life will not guarantee you are free from pain or hardship. It does guarantee you will never face situations alone again. You have stuffed fears and feelings down for years. Some of you have stayed in a relationship for years and remained miserable. Others have had the courage to leave but found you repeated the same old patterns – again. Once you understand these patterns, you can heal. It is time to build a foundation of forgiveness. This allows you to grow beyond your past so it does not repeat.
Forgiveness	You must forgive those who hurt you. Have you ever heard the saying, *"Anger destroys the vessel it is in."*? If you do not forgive those who hurt you, you will be the one that hurts. Forgiveness does not mean that it erases what that person did to you. Forgiveness stops you from holding on to the past so God can fill you with the next opportunity.
Bitter or Better?	Will you become bitter or better? The root of bitterness produces fruit of anger and hatred. Bitterness will cost you future blessings and take things out of your life you cannot get back. *"See to it that no one falls short of the grace of God and that no bitter root grows up to cause trouble and defile many."* — **Hebrews 12:15 (NIV)**

Continued on next page

Chapter 9: Powerless, Forgiveness, Bitterness, Continued

God helps us forgive

God has a clear message on forgiveness:

1. God made it clear we need to forgive:

   "⁹ Our Father in heaven, Hallowed by Your name. ¹⁰ Your kingdom come, Your will be done. On earth as it is in heaven. ¹¹ Give us this day our daily bread. ¹² And forgive us our debts, As we forgive our debtors. ¹³ And do not lead us into temptation, But deliver us from the evil one, For Yours is the kingdom and the power and the glory forever. Amen.   **— Matthew 6:9–13 (NKJV)**

2. We must forgive others:

   "²³Therefore if you bring your gift to the altar, and there remember that your brother has something against you, ²⁴ leave your gift there before the altar, and go your way. First be reconciled to your brother, and then come and offer your gift."
                                   — Matthew 5:23, 24 (NKJV)

3. Forgive our enemies, for that is when you can truly be free:

   "But I say to you, love your enemies, bless those who curse you, do good to those who hate you, and pray for those who spitefully use you and persecute you."
                                   — Matthew 5:44 (NKJV)

4. God tells us that he will give us the patience to forgive:

   "A man's wisdom gives him patience, it is to his glory to overlook an offense."
                                   — Proverbs 19:11(NIV)

- Who do you need to forgive and why?

- What holds you back?

- What is the first step you can take to forgive?

Continued on next page

Chapter 9: Powerless, Forgiveness, Bitterness, Continued

Self-forgiveness

The last segment of Chapter 9 is to forgive yourself. Self-forgiveness can be one of the most difficult things to do and it comes in layers. We recognize that God has forgiven us, but we still struggle to forgive ourselves. We say we do, but then we pick it back up again and begin self-condemnation, worthlessness, self-doubt, fear, etc..

The hardest forgiveness

Forgiving others is hard, but forgiving ourselves can feel impossible.

How do you forgive yourself?

"You don't understand, I've made so many mistakes."

"I just can't get over it."

"I don't know why I did that."

"I am so ashamed."

It takes time

Forgiving yourself takes time. It is not an overnight fix. Months, years can go by and you still feel the "twang" in your gut from the hurt.

Often the guilt can get worse as you get further away from the abusive lifestyle. You begin to see how you covered up, lied and made choices that made sense at the time; but no longer seem appropriate.

Forgiveness is often your regret. Sadness that you did….or did not …

God's beat you to it

God has already forgiven all your transgressions.

"As far as the east is from the west, So far has He removed our transgressions from us."

— Psalms 103:12 (NKJV)

Continued on next page

Chapter 9: Powerless, Forgiveness, Bitterness, Continued

Jesus and Peter   Jesus tells a story about true forgiveness and how much he loves us no matter what. We know Jesus forgives us, so it helps us ease up and realize that we too can forgive ourselves.

Peter was one of Jesus' twelve disciples and the night of that last supper Jesus took great care with them washing their feet and being humble in their presence. Jesus tells Peter that before the night is over he will deny him three times. Peter says, *"No way, God, that can't be true. I love you."* Later that night Peter denies Jesus three times.

How would you have liked to deny the Savior?

Would you feel guilty and ashamed that you lied about him to others?

Peter was left with a pretty heavy burden to carry for the rest of his life.

Did Jesus hold a grudge? No.

He came to Peter in the ocean. He loved him. He invited him to come have breakfast together. Then he asked, *"Do you love me?"* Peter replied, *"Yes,"* Jesus gave him another chance and asked him to be a fisher of men and serve Him.

Jesus accepted Peter with open arms despite what he did in the past. Jesus gave Peter three chances to make right for each time Peter denied Him. Jesus is the God of second, third and 'seven times seventy' opportunities to redeem ourselves and reclaim our life through Him. Hallelujah!

Read this story in your Bible: John 13:6, 13:38, 18:25–27, 21:12, 21:15.

Have you ever felt like Peter?

Continued on next page

Chapter 9: Powerless, Forgiveness, Bitterness, Continued

Release regrets

"He who covers his sins will not prosper, but whoever confesses and forsakes them will have mercy."   **— Proverbs 28:13 (NKJV)**

"Therefore confess your sins to each other and pray for each other so that you may be healed. The prayer of a righteous person is powerful and effective."   **— James 5:16 (NKJV)**

Releasing regrets is a part of your forgiveness process.

1.   What do you regret?

2.   List areas in your life where you feel shame or guilt?

3.   Describe your life if you were able to let that regret go?

4.   What steps can you take to make that possible?

Stop, Drop and Roll

Three easy steps to self-forgiveness.

Stop. Drop and Roll.

1.   Stop regrets.
2.   Drop to your knees in prayer.
3.   Roll to keep you from the fire of self-hatred that destroys all God wants you to be.

Continued on next page

Chapter 9: Powerless, Forgiveness, Bitterness, Continued

Pray to fill the holes

When we fill the holes prayer will be a lifeline and can sooth those hurts. Sometimes we don't know exactly how to pray or what to pray for. There is no wrong way to pray. Spending time with God is the key and will allow you to grow from there.

Here is a sample prayer you can use for a guideline if you like:

Lord I thank you Heavenly Father for this opportunity to serve you. I ask for your Holy Spirit to come now and cover me.

Anoint me and protect me Lord.

I ask you now Lord that you fill my holes now Lord.

Fill the hole of (specifically name the emotion or hurt: anger, fear, sexual abuse, pain, etc.) with your joy and amazing grace. Leave me noticeably changed from your presence.

Let me forgive those (or insert specific name(s)) that hurt me in my past.

I ask forgiveness for my sins and all resentment and anger to be released. Fill me with your love and grace Lord.

Now Father I forgive myself.

Protect us Father and in your name we pray. Amen.

Audience tip: When each woman finishes praying in your group you can add: *Your word says when two or more are together we can ask a "thing" and it shall be.*

Continued on next page

Chapter 9: Powerless, Forgiveness, Bitterness, Continued

Write your own   Write your own forgiveness prayer. Forgive them. Forgive yourself.

Notes:

Chapter 10: Types of Abuse, Cycles, Safety, Legal

Purpose
Chapter 10 helps you know how to identify abuse, categorize behaviors into types of abuse, recognize the cycle of abuse in your life and seek appropriate help if necessary.

Where does it occur?
Domestic violence has many forms, including physical violence, sexual domination, emotional trauma, social isolation or economic restrictions. [33]

Domestic violence occurs in all cultures, ethnicities, races, religions, and in all socioeconomic levels.

Victims of domestic violence can be both men and women, and can occur in same-sex and opposite-sex relationships. In some cases throughout this text, there are references to abuse using masculine pronouns for writing purposes only, and does not try to limit or suggest that only males can be abusers. Abusers can be anyone regardless of gender, sexual orientation, age, physical size, body strength. They are often in a relationship with the victim and can be family, friend, neighbor, coworker or other close tie.

Definition: Domestic abuse
Domestic violence is defined as, "abusive behavior – emotional, psychological, physical, or sexual – that one person in an intimate relationship uses in order to control the other." [34]

Abuse escalates

"Years of emotional and verbal abuse finally escalated to physical abuse, and I had to go to the emergency room for treatment."

Continued on next page

Chapter 10: Types of Abuse, Cycles, Safety, Legal, Continued

Physical abuse   Physical violence can be both Direct and Indirect:

Physical abuse — Direct

- Hits, slaps, punches or kicks.
- Shoves or chokes.
- Restrains you or keeps you from leaving.
- Rapes you or sexually controls you.
- Locks you out of the house or car.
- Abandons you in a dangerous place.
- Refuses to help you when you are sick, injured or pregnant.
- Subjects you to reckless behavior while driving or at home.
- Threatens to hurt you with a weapon.

Physical abuse — Indirect

- Abuses your pets.
- Throws objects at you.
- Breaks furniture, belongings, personal effects.
- Forces you to break the law; shoplift, sell drugs or sell your body.
- Makes you submissive by threatening to go to the authorities or immigration.
- Withholds important personal papers, passport or immigration documents.
- Withholds medicine you require.[35]

Continued on next page

Chapter 10: Types of Abuse, Cycles, Safety, Legal, Continued

Just to cope

"To cope with the abuse I was experiencing, often my soul would separate from my body. So that I could remove myself from the "machine gun spray" of words. My skin transformed into an empty shell and my inner soul would dissociate to escape from the abuse.

Unfortunately, instead of removing myself from this situation, by creating a survival technique, I became emotionally numb which perpetuated the abuse. Later, I learned this was how I survived the abuse so I could be free from the blame.

Emotional abuse

This form of abuse is very common and can be one of the worst forms. When there is no physical violence, many victims do not recognize what they endure as abuse. They, and others, make excuses to justify the verbal lashings.

Emotional abuse erodes self-esteem and can do long-lasting damage to the mental, emotional and physical state of the individual. It can act as a silent destroyer because it is able to be sustained for long periods of time.

Over time you are emotionally worn down by your abuser. The way you are treated becomes your new "normal" and your objectivity diminishes and you lose sight of how destructive this pattern is in your life.

The abuser uses tactics of blame, criticism, intimidation and verbal harassment to destroy your sense of safety, self-esteem, and self-worth. Often the abuser lies and manipulates the truth, so you become confused and have nowhere to turn. This form of abuse destroys your sense of individuality and personal value and increases the power of the abuse.[36] Then you become afraid, alone, embarrassed, helpless and guilty.

Some victims have described that they have felt their life force was being "sucked up" or "drained away" by their abuser.

Continued on next page

Chapter 10: Types of Abuse, Cycles, Safety, Legal, Continued

Emotional abuse (continued)

Emotional abuse can be Verbal or Non-verbal: [37]

Verbal —

- Criticizes you alone or in public.
- Shouts at you.
- Humiliates you or pokes fun at you.
- Insults your beliefs, religion, race, heritage or social class.
- Speech, jokes, and stories are demeaning to women as a group.
- Threatens to leave you or says you will be leaving.
- Punishes children when you don't comply.
- Threatens to kidnap children if you leave.
- Tells lies to manipulate you.
- Says you are the one that is crazy.
- Subjects you to violent mood swings, keeps you on an emotional roller coaster.
- Constantly criticizing what you do and how you do it.
- Calls you "stupid," "incapable," "inadequate".
- Tells others and your children what a bad parent you are.
- Insults, put downs, or criticizes you in public.
- Complains about your physical appearance making you feel inadequate.
- Threatens to take you to court.
- Blames others.

Continued on next page

Chapter 10: Types of Abuse, Cycles, Safety, Legal, Continued

Emotional abuse (continued)

Non-verbal —

- Using "the look" to scare you or to bring you into submission.

- Grits teeth or grimaces at you.

- Shake fists or fingers at you.

- Stands close or in an overbearing way.

- Blocks access to door or means of escape.

- Ignores you.

- Punishes by withholding approval, appreciation or affection.

- Withholds praise or good feelings from you.

Brainwashed

"Emotional abuse can be compared with intentional brainwashing. Emotional abusers usually leave the victim confused, weak, depressed, angry, and numb with unclear thinking — and yet loyal to their abusers, hoping the abusive behavior will change...Emotional abuse can produce scars that will remain with you for years." [38]

Continued on next page

Chapter 10: Types of Abuse, Cycles, Safety, Legal, Continued

Sexual abuse   Signs of Sexual abuse: [39]

- Harasses you about having an affair.
- Stalks you during your daily activities.
- Disrespects women in general, or other family members.
- Demands you dress in a way that you are not comfortable with.
- Does not care about your feelings toward sex.
- Criticizes you sexually either alone or in public.
- Forces you to perform sexual acts you are not comfortable performing.
- Withholds sex and affection.
- Calls you sexual names like "whore" or "frigid" in private or public.
- Forces you to undress when you do not want to undress.
- Shows sexual interest in other women.
- Has affairs after agreeing to a monogamous relationship.
- Forces sex when you are sick or it is a danger to your health.
- Forces sex for the purpose of hurting you with objects or weapons
- Commits sadistic sexual acts.
- Rapes you or coerces you sexually.
- Requires you to watch or engage in pornography when you are not interested.

Continued on next page

Chapter 10: Types of Abuse, Cycles, Safety, Legal, Continued

Social abuse   Signs of Social abuse: [40]

- Restricts your ability to work or volunteer for social interaction.

- Limits contact with your family or friends.

- Harasses or punishes you for having friends, makes fun of them, interrogates you and often makes it so difficult that you end the relationship.

- Physically moves you away from a familiar location or area where you have an established social network.

- Friends of abuser are chemically dependent.

- You feel like a prisoner.

- Not allowed to schedule your own time.

- Won't let you socialize with others and/or won't take you out.

- Does not allow you to take the car alone.

Continued on next page

Chapter 10: Types of Abuse, Cycles, Safety, Legal, Continued

Financial abuse   Financial abuse signs: [41]

- Provides 100% or the majority of the income for the household and uses that fact to control, intimidate or manipulate.

- Restricts you from working.

- Refuses to work leaving finances strained and unbearable.

- Keeps the family in debt.

- Causes trouble for you at work which can lead to embarrassment or disciplinary action by your employer or even termination.

- Forces you to work at a job you dislike.

- Allows no access to money or resources.

- Assets are controlled by abuser.

- As a punishment or to force you to comply to their request, they take control or withdraw all family money leaving you struggling.

- No independent access to money.

- You are kept pregnant and not allowed access to birth control when you have requested it.

- Abuser threatens you with divorce or that he will not let you get a divorce.

Continued on next page

Chapter 10: Types of Abuse, Cycles, Safety, Legal, Continued

Still with your abuser

If you are still with your abuser:

1. If you are in immediate danger or your life is at risk call 9-1-1.

2. The outcomes are often unknown while living with an abuser. Seek help and do not do this alone. Your safety is very important.

3. You can call a crisis line in your local area that will give you resources in your community.

4. Contact family centers, battered women shelters, crisis centers in your area.

5. You can call your local police or sheriff's office and ask them to direct you to someone who can help you about domestic abuse.

6. If you have safe access to the internet search for domestic abuse + your city or county, and you will find many resources that are in your area and a wealth of reading material to help educate you. Local libraries have free internet access.

7. If you have been involved with the court system, the State Attorney's office has a Victim's Advocate and counseling programs that are available free of charge to guide you through this educational and your recovery phase.

Even if you are physically separated from the abuser, you may still feel they are trying to control and abuse you:

1. Recognizing the behavior you endured as abusive is important. Their incorrect behavior allows you to be free from guilt. You did not cause it. You cannot do anything better to make it improve.

2. Start connecting with people: Stronger than Espresso®, church activities or individuals with similar interests.

Chapter 10: Types of Abuse, Cycles, Safety, Legal, Continued

Identify commonalities

Coming to terms with the abuse can be shocking, debilitating, and even sickening. This is the beginning of your long journey.

From the previous lists of types of abuse, answer the following questions:

- After reviewing the various types of abuse, which ones stand out the most?

- Which ones have reoccurred in multiple relationships you have had?

- List any abuses that you remember observing from your home growing up?

- In your next relationship how will you establish boundaries so these do not occur?

Continued on next page

Chapter 10: Types of Abuse, Cycles, Safety, Legal, Continued

Who has control

Control impacts my relationships:

- Who has control over you in your life?

- Describe how this person(s) make you feel?

- What would be the risk if you asked them to stop treating you a certain way?

Continued on next page

Chapter 10: Types of Abuse, Cycles, Safety, Legal, Continued

God's intention

Healthy relationships are designed differently. Unfortunately, many of us who experience abuse as adults experienced abuse as a child. Healthy and normal were not words we would have used to describe our family relationships growing up.

Healthy relationships are full of love, respect, kindness and a mutual agreement that each person is an individual. Each individual has the right to have boundaries, the right to say Yes or No, and the ability to live in an environment free from this type of abuse.

What love is it supposed to be:

> *Love is long suffering and kind. Love is not jealous, it does not brag, does not get puffed up, does not behave indecently, does not look for its own interests, does not become provoked. It does not keep account of injury. It does not rejoice over unrighteousness, but rejoices with the truth. It bears all things, believes all things, hopes all things, endures all things. Love never fails...*
> **— 1 Corinthians 13:4–8 (NLT)**

- Describe people, places or events that have made you feel you received this kind of love?

- To whom can you show this kind of love?

- What is holding you back from loving yourself like this?

Continued on next page

Chapter 10: Types of Abuse, Cycles, Safety, Legal, Continued

Healthy Relationship Comparison

Review the comparison of healthy to unhealthy relationships:[42]

Area	Type of Abuse	Unhealthy Relationship	Healthy Relationships
Children	Emotional	Use children to promote guilt, threaten, transfer adult information, elicit fear of their safety.	Responsible parenting. Does not use children for abuse or manipulation. Shares parental responsibilities. Positive role model for children.
Criticism, Put Downs, Talking Incessantly	Emotional	Repeated negative criticism, unrealistic expectations cannot be met, always under achieving, disrespectful, no quiet time given for you to rest or think.	Honor and respect you in private, and in front of others. Does not make fun of you. Agree on expectations and set mutual goals and understanding. Respects your need for quiet time.
Financial	Economic and Emotional	Prevents you from getting or keeping a job, controls finances, takes your money.	Economic partnership. Money decisions are shared.
Interrogation	Emotional	Excessive questioning based on abuser's fears. Being pulled through the "interrogation funnel." When they begin they will not let up; keep badgering.	Honesty. Questions are based out of interest, no need to manipulate, control or trap.
Isolation	Emotional	Attempts to control what you see, when you go out, who you see, who you talk to, what you read and where you go. Based by jealousy, criticism and fear.	Supports your goals, respects your right to your own activities, feelings, friends and opinions. Mutual trust and support.
Mental Games	Emotional	Confusing behavior. Kindness followed by cruelty. Lying and manipulation. Continuous state of chaos. Says that "you are crazy." Blames you for their actions or for all the problems in relationship.	Consistent behavior and expectations. Honest communication.

Continued on next page

Chapter 10: Types of Abuse, Cycles, Safety, Legal, Continued

Areas	Type of Abuse	Unhealthy Relationship	Healthy Relationship
Physical Threats	Physical	Uses fists, body language, gestures or weapons to encourage or force submissive behavior.	Negotiate mutually agreed compromises. No threats necessary.
Power and Control	Emotional	Treats you like a servant. Does not allow you the ability to make choices.	Shared responsibility. Work together to distribute work. One party is not more powerful than the other.
Pushing or Shoving	Physical	Pushes or shoves out of frustration, anger or power.	No one has the right to push or shove another person.
Responsibility	Emotional	Shifts responsibility to abused. Accuses, blames others, and twists truth.	Accepts responsibility for own actions by being truthful when wrong.
Sexual	Sexual	Rape, force inappropriate or unwanted sexual acts.	No one has the right to force sexual activity on any other person.
Time	Emotional	Obsessed: Jealousy or stalking. Preoccupied with your thoughts and whereabouts. Neglect: Ignores you. Does not have time or interest in you.	Healthy interest in you and your activities. Allows you space and freedom to balance individual and relationship demands. Eager to spend time-sharing your thoughts and interests.
Verbal Threats	Emotional	Make threats to: Hurt you or your family. Leave you. Cut off money. Divorce you or refuse to divorce. Discredit you. Take you back to court.	Negotiation, fairness and safety. Compromise with no threats. Reach resolutions to conflict that are good for both parties.

Table 2. Healthy Relationship Comparison.   Source: Stronger than Espresso, Inc. © 2014.

Continued on next page

Chapter 10: Types of Abuse, Cycles, Safety, Legal, Continued

Reprogram

You can't change them. The individual must decide to change.

Work on yourself and pray for God to change your life.

You can also pray for the abuser as a part of your act of forgiveness. You may need time to be emotionally and spiritually ready for this step — don't rush it.

If the abuser sincerely requests for God's grace to move in their life they too can find freedom from their need to control others in unhealthy ways. This, however, is between them and God.

You are not responsible for their recovery.

- Identify warning signs you have experienced in past or current relationship.

- Compare those to the healthy/unhealthy behaviors chart. Describe how your relationship would be different if you expected only healthy behaviors.

- Imagine if God planned your relationships and your healthy partner. What standards and guidelines would He establish?

Making the shift to loving and healthy relationships can be hard when you are still in an unhealthy pattern, struggle with love addiction or just can't stick to your "No." You may know the signs and red flags, but not willing to accept them in someone you care about. Often justification of another's behavior can occur in this lesson. You should not have to justify behavior. Self-check by seeking wisdom. Ask your Stronger than Espresso Sisters about the signs you see in this other person and ask their objective point of view.

Continued on next page

Chapter 10: Types of Abuse, Cycles, Safety, Legal, Continued

Cycles of abuse	In abusive relationships, you repeat an abuse cycle. This process becomes the new blueprint of how you act, react and interact in your relationships. The longer this cycle continues you become more engrained into this perpetuating the cycle. If you are unable to recognize this pattern when it occurs, you lose perspective and become unaware of the repetitiveness.
What is the Cycle of Violence?	Lenore Walker, a legend in the field of domestic violence, constructed the model of the Cycle of Violence which consists of three basic phases: [43]
Phase 1	**Tension Building Phase** — Characterized by poor communication, tension and fear of the next outburst. Minor battery incidents. Increased tension and anger. Blame and prone to argue. Victim denies own anger at being unjustifiably hurt. Time length variable.
Phase 2	**Acting Out Phase** — Characterized by outburst of violent abusive incidents. Battering, including hitting, slapping, kicking, choking, use of objects or weapons. Verbal threats and abuse, including sexual abuse. Time length 2–24 hours, maybe longer.
Phase 3	**Honeymoon Phase** — Characterized by affection, apology and apparent end of violence. Period of calm. Victim believes abuser can change. Time period is unknown but tends to decrease over time.

Continued on next page

Chapter 10: Types of Abuse, Cycles, Safety, Legal, Continued

Let's break down the cycle even more:

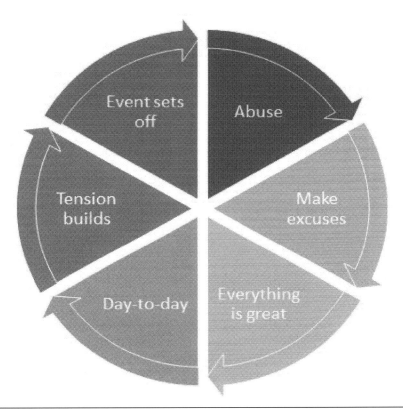

Figure 8. Abusive Relationship Cycle.   Source: Stronger than Espresso, Inc. © 2014.

After reviewing the circle diagram above, describe similarities to your own relationships in each stage of the Cycle. You will find when you discuss your experiences with other women who have also been abused, you will have experiences in common.

Continued on next page

Chapter 10: Types of Abuse, Cycles, Safety, Legal, Continued

How the process continues: [44]

Abuser	Victim
The paradox exists, because the abuser does not want to face the fact that his problems are within himself.	Accepting the blame becomes the specific purpose of the victim.
This denial allows the abuser to blame someone else for his emotions, feelings and actions.	The victim will accept blame to survive, and will operate from the theory that if they can make the abuse happen, they can also make it stop. That is not true.
The abuser has an emotional attachment to the victim that is not love.	The victim does not create the abuse and does not have the power to make it stop.
They have an unhealthy dependency to reinforce blame and avoid accepting responsibility for his actions.	When you have been a victim of this type of relationship for a long period of time or had numerous relationships with these characteristics, you are not experiencing true love from another person.
Only way to make it stop: Abuser accepts responsibility for his actions.	**Only way to make it stop:** Victim must stop accepting blame.

Table 3. How the Abuse Process Continues.   Source: Stronger than Espresso, Inc. © 2014.

Your new standard	The whirlwind romance followed by a roller-coaster relationship is not healthy. Set new standards for healthy relationships. Accept nothing less.

Continued on next page

Chapter 10: Types of Abuse, Cycles, Safety, Legal, Continued

Oh no, not again!

"Once away from the emotional and physical abuse, I sought support and tried to trust new people. Being raw, weak, and vulnerable, I played right into the hands of another person who was a new type of abuser. This person gained my trust, and then stole financially from me during the time I was trying to rebuild.

During those few years it all seemed to make sense why I was giving all my money away to this individual, but it left me financially captive in another bad situation. I found it almost impossible to believe that this individual could be hurting me when I thought I finally built a bond that was safe. It took physically moving away from this person to release me from this situation, and a long time before I could admit that I was used; again!"

Warning signs

Batterers have common behaviors that are warning signs you should know. If you are currently dating or meet someone with these red flag behaviors, know there is a strong potential for violence. The more signs the person has, the more likely they are to be a batterer.

Remember that abuse escalates. What might be limited to emotional and/or verbal abuse can easily escalate.

Think about a small child's behavior when they get angry. He/she may throw a toy across the room when they get frustrated. When an adult maintains these childish behaviors and does not "get their way," this can mean violence directed towards you when they are frustrated.

Continued on next page

Chapter 10: Types of Abuse, Cycles, Safety, Legal, Continued

What to look for

Be aware of abuser characteristics and know what people to avoid: [45]

- Blames you or others for his bad mood.

- Blames you or others for inappropriate behavior.

- Breaks or strikes objects.

- Constantly manipulates you, other people or situations.

- Controls whom you speak to, when you go places, where you go, what you do and how you get there.

- Cuts you off from friends, coworkers, family and neighbors.

- During an argument they hold, restrain, push or shove.

- Easy to anger or easy to be hurt by others.

- Terrorizes others into submission when angry.

- History of battery exists.

- Isolates you from resources: money, food, social interaction.

- Is jealous or stalks, calls constantly, visits unexpectedly, checks mileage.

- Masterful at fooling others of the truth; may even brag on how easy it was to manipulate, lie or cheat someone else.

- Needs to know your whereabouts.

- No concern for your desire for sex; holds you down, forces you to perform acts you are not comfortable with. Manipulates you so you will comply; makes fun or criticizes you sexually.

- Polite and charming to others. Different behavior at home that no one sees.

- Pressures you to commit to the relationship right away, even if you are not ready.

- Questions excessively; interrogation.

- Sudden changes in mood from ecstatic to explosive.

Continued on next page

Chapter 10: Types of Abuse, Cycles, Safety, Legal, Continued

What to look for (continued)	• Thinks people are out to get him or are plotting against him.
	• Threatens you or your loved ones in any manner.
	• Whirlwind romance; requires quick commitment.
	• Will not accept responsibility for mistakes made.
	• Criticizes you because you are unable to meet all their needs or be the perfect mate.
	• You do not feel safe leaving them alone with your child or pet.
	• You do not feel safe with them when they are angry.
	• You feel they are cruel to your pet or your child.
	• Your sense of safety has eroded or disappeared.
	• Excessive texting, found spyware on your computer, demands your online passwords.
	• Is cruel, demeans or frightens you when you are sick, vulnerable or pregnant.
	Describe characteristics that sound familiar.

Abusers desire control	The abuser has an intense desire to control. The victim helps the abuser continue to feel that his/her problems are not within himself/herself. When the victim is not available, the abuser often gets upset and experiences guilt and depression. The abuser is most likely to become most violent if the victim threatens or attempts to leave.

Continued on next page

Chapter 10: Types of Abuse, Cycles, Safety, Legal, Continued

Safety Plan

If you are considering making a change to a relationship, or have made a recent change in the past, you should have a safety plan. No matter how long you have been out of the relationship there is always a need for safety. All women should have emergency contact and resource numbers.

Danger assessment

Answer the following questions, Yes or No:

	Yes/No
1. Do you have a feeling or intuition that your partner is going to hurt you?	
2. Has your partner threatened to commit suicide, kill you, your children, pets or other family member?	
3. Does your partner have a history of suicide attempts?	
4. Is your partner's behavior escalating? More reckless, scary or violent?	
5. Your partner has weapons and has used them to threaten you or others?	
6. Drug or alcohol use is escalating? When under the influence is their behavior more abusive, intense, paranoid, or suspicious?	
7. Does your partner harass you stating they know you are going to leave?	
8. Are you afraid they will kill you?	
9. Are you seriously considering suicide as a way out?	
10. Are you fantasizing of your partner being killed or dying knowing then the abuse will stop?	
11. Is your partner suffering from delusions or hearing voices?	
12. Has your partner just experienced a new significant loss: a death, loss of job, legal trouble, illness?	
13. Have you just experienced a new significant loss?	
14. Have you been attacked by your partner while pregnant?	
15. Your partner has stopped fearing future arrests or legal ramifications from abusive or criminal activity?	

Continued on next page

Chapter 10: Types of Abuse, Cycles, Safety, Legal, Continued

Danger assessment (continued)

Review your answers. The more Yes answers you have, the higher your present danger. Should you have any Yes answers you should take caution and seek out the help and advice from a counselor, therapist, pastor, or visit a women's shelter in your local area. [46] Take this very seriously and find help with a counselor, women's shelter, church or talk to a trusted friend. Let someone know your situation.

Safety plan

Once you have identified that you are in an abusive relationship and assessed your danger, you must take caution and build your safety plan.

Prior to your "aha moment," you would play your part in the cycle of violence perfectly and your abuser could count on it. Once you start to realize that this behavior is not okay, it is human nature to want to stop it. Be careful that you do not try a method that is not safe and smart.

Be patient and think about what you are doing before you do anything. Your danger level at this time is extremely high. Remember: educate before you activate.

I am out of danger

No matter how long you have been away from the relationship, protecting your safety should always be a priority. Time often does not change their need to control those around them. You may not be aware of their need to bring you back into their circle of control. Even creating a modified version of a full safety plan will keep you and your family safe for years to come.

You may have a friend, family member, neighbor or coworker that is an abusive relationship. Be prepared to give them the advice, help and support they need too.

Continued on next page

Chapter 10: Types of Abuse, Cycles, Safety, Legal, Continued

Generate your safety plan

It is now time to construct your safety plan.

List important phone numbers and addresses and keep it in a safe place. Include emergency numbers, local police or sheriff, shelter crisis lines, family members, friends, work associates, legal advocate, children's day care, baby sitter, school and doctor offices. [47] Below is a chart to use as a guideline:

Emergency	9-1-1	National Domestic Violence Hotline	800-799-SAFE 800-799-7233
Police / Fire	( )	Local crisis line or shelter number	( ) ( ) ( )
Work	( )	Family	( )
Supervisor's cell	( )	Family	( )
Physician	( )	Family	( )
Pediatrician	( )	Friend	( )
Child School	( )	Friend	( )
Baby Sitter	( )	Friend	( )
Workmate	( )	Workmate	( )
Neighbor	( )	Neighbor	( )

Continued on next page

Chapter 10: Types of Abuse, Cycles, Safety, Legal, Continued

Steps to take

- Plan the escape route from home and practice it. Know that you have a safe place for you and your children in an emergency.

- Teach children how to use an emergency phone. Keep prepaid phone card in a safe place. Go to a women's shelter and ask for a free cell phone to call 9-1-1 if necessary.

- Ask trusted neighbors, family and friends to listen, watch and call for help if they see suspicious activities around or near your home.

- Create a code word to with friends and family when you need help.

- When violence erupts, avoid the kitchen, bathroom and any room without a door to the outside.

- Make sure all locks and lights work inside and out.

- Ask yourself, is there anyone you can trust. Select a person you trust outside you and your partner's circle of friends. Share with them your need to have a safety plan.

- Find a safe place to keep an emergency kit outside of home and car. Keep it either at your work or with a trusted friend.

- Recommended items to keep in your Emergency Kit:

• ID / Passport	• Birth certificate	• ATM card/ checks
• Social security card	• Food stamps, Medicaid card	• Health care ID
• Extra house key	• Extra car key	• Medical records
• School records	• Copies of joint bills / loans	• Proof of partner's income
• Copies of legal papers / Injunctions	• Car registration	• Prepaid long distance card
• Change of clothes	• Prescriptions	• Personal hygiene (toothpaste, toothbrush, shampoo, lotion)
• Keepsakes, photographs	• Formula / diapers	• Recent photograph and personal information of abuser, auto, work phone, addresses etc.
• Bottled water and non-perishable foods items	• cell phone	• Cash

Continued on next page

Chapter 10: Types of Abuse, Cycles, Safety, Legal, Continued

Safety plan at work

Domestic violence does not always remain in the home and can present situations at work that are not only embarrassing, but can be dangerous. Working requires routine, specific drive times, and an established driving route. Be alert and aware that if the abuser wants to find you, they can. Typically they may contact you during the workday or on your way to and from work. If you can, attempt to follow the suggestions below. Disruptions at work could cause you to put your job at risk.

Review the following tips: [48]

- Notify boss or coworker of the situation and give them instructions on what to do if you do not show up for work.

- Make sure your boss is aware that if you do not show up on time that they should contact you to check if there is a problem. Make certain you make a point to be at work on time every day, or if you will be late make sure to communicate so they do not worry or overreact.

- Ask someone to watch out for you when you enter and exit the building.

- If needed, keep your emergency kit in your desk at work.

- Keep a copy of the injunction at work. Keep a photograph of the abuser in case something happens.

- Request use of the Employee Assistance Program (EAP). If your employer has this benefit, it typically offers six visits of free counseling.

- Plan an escape route from the building.

- Carry a whistle and have a signal.

- Vary your route to and from work and change where you park each day.

Continued on next page

Chapter 10: Types of Abuse, Cycles, Safety, Legal, Continued

Safety while on your own

Once you are separated from the abuser you still need to maintain your safety. Review the list below and incorporate into your safety plan:

- Continue to have a Safety Plan at home and work as you did before. Review them now and update paperwork and phone numbers if items changed since you moved.

- Visit a local women's shelter and request an emergency cellular telephone if available.

- Make sure all locks and lights work.

- If you can, install simple alarms on windows and doors.

- Secure windows and sliding glass doors with wood or pole.

- Install smoke detector and get fire extinguisher. Contact your local fire department and ask if they have a free installation program. Often you can buy the detector and extinguisher at a discount through the fire department and they will install and test for free.

- Get an unlisted telephone number.

- Receive mail at a PO Box and do not file a forward or change of address with the post office. This information is not private and easy to access where you moved. Instead change your address with each vendor individually.

- Get an Injunction for Protection.

- If you put utilities in your name your address is now easy to access. Any attorney, private eye or small fee internet investigative company can pull that information on you. If you can, and if necessary, put utilities in a friend's name.

- Are you being tracked with a GPS tracking device? Does your vehicle have a GPS tracking device? There are many GPS tracking devices and they come in many forms. If you or your kids have been given any presents they may contain a tracking device?

  Accounts can be activated or GPS initiated by the abuser for tracking if their name is on the account or car title.

Continued on next page

Chapter 10: Types of Abuse, Cycles, Safety, Legal, Continued

**Safety while
on your own**
(continued)

- Are you being watched? Hidden cameras come in many different forms? They may be installed in your home and you unaware

- Do they seem to know everything you say? Cell phones can be put in auto answer, silent mode and act like a simple "bug." They can be hidden in your home or car without your knowledge.

- Immediately, put a verbal password on cellular phone, banking, and credit card accounts.

- Contact your cellular phone, banking and credit card companies and confirm all your contact information, specifically your email address. If you do not have email make sure that you have a verbal password on these accounts so that none can be added without your knowledge.

  It is very easy for someone to call, pretend to be you, request to add or update your email address, activate or reset online account services. Online they request a new password be sent to the new email they noted on your account. Once logged into your account, they can print statements, view current activity, track you, or harass people you are talking to. They can remove the email just as easily and you may never know that it was done.

  Make sure to protect all accounts with a verbal password so updates like that cannot be done without your knowledge.

- Remember this individual typically has all your personal information, social security, family history, address history, and password histories. Change your security questions or mother's maiden name to a word that only you know so you are protected. Change all passwords to a word or letter combination you have never used before.

- Remember that when you sign a lease on an apartment a credit check is conducted which will show on your credit report. If they pull a simple background check report from the internet they can find it.

- When you change your address with your credit card companies, this information and your new address will be boldly listed on your credit report. If you were married or had joint credit, your new address may be displayed on his report too.

Continued on next page

Chapter 10: Types of Abuse, Cycles, Safety, Legal, Continued

Safety While on Your Own *(continued)*

- You can have your mail sent to domestic violence center and forwarded to you if you must. Make sure to be in contact with your local crisis center to discuss how they can help you.

  Keep a log and record any communication from the abuser.

- Do not communicate or retaliate with the abuser. This can be very difficult as they will try any means to get you to call them back, meet them, help them or see them.

  Remember, they are a master manipulator who receives power by actions and words directed at you. You do not have to talk to them. Sometimes it seems easier to just get it over with when you are being harassed, but communication just perpetuates the game in their mind. They do not want to be ignored and they do not want to face their problems without you to blame.

- In extreme cases you can change your social security number, but requires assistance with your local crisis center. When you do this your credit history is deleted and your accumulation of your payments into Social Security (your ten quarters) is voided, which would cancel your benefits available at retirement. Recognize that they can "find you" with many other means than your social security number so think very carefully before pursuing this option.

- Make an appointment with your medical doctor and tell them what is going on. This documents your situation. The medical doctor may give you a prescription to visit a counselor and it may be covered by insurance. They also can prescribe medication for this transition time making it easier for you to cope with the stress. You will be full of fear, anxiety and may not be sleeping or thinking clearly. It is important to listen to their medical advice.

- Do not resort to alcohol, sex with strangers, drugs or any other behavior during this time no matter how much you can justify it. Keep your wits about you. This is vital to your success in this transition. Learn how to live with yourself. Yes — you will make yourself crazy, but it is only for now. Abstain. Practice self-respect. Love yourself just as you are.

Continued on next page

Chapter 10: Types of Abuse, Cycles, Safety, Legal, Continued

**Make your
safety plan**

Describe the safety plans you need to make?

Make a list of the items you need to complete this week to ensure your safety:

-
-
-
-
-

Continued on next page

Chapter 10: Types of Abuse, Cycles, Safety, Legal, Continued

God is with you in trouble

Reading Bible verses can be very valuable when you are feeling in trouble, insecure or afraid. You can locate resources in the Bible to help comfort you when you going through a difficult time.

Read the verses below and describe what the Bible speaks to your heart through the holy spirit.

Psalms Book	What does this verse speak to you?
Psalms 27	
Psalms 28	
Psalms 37	
Psalms 102	

Describe how God is with you in trouble?

Continued on next page

Chapter 10: Types of Abuse, Cycles, Safety, Legal, Continued

What about them?

If you are asking the question, "Can they change?" you are evaluating the relationship at some level. If the person you are with is abusive they will need to dedicate to the work required to change. Working with a professional counselor, enrolling in programs like an anger management programs and counseling specifically designed for abusers individuals is a must for the abusive patterns to have a chance to stop.

Can the abuser change?

Can the abuser change? Yes, but only if they seek help, admit their problem and commit to a lifelong change of their behavior. Anything less, they will fail and fall back into old habits. For change to be successful, the abuser must prove <u>all</u> the following criteria:

- Admission — Abusers must admit their problem. Identifying the problem is the first step to correcting it. Without this step, there will be no change. Blaming you or something else is not admission.

- Ask for Help — The abuser must request professional assistance. The counseling must be individual at first, and then later can include marital or group counseling. Violence as a solution to a problem is not acceptable. There is no need for marital counseling until the abuser can respond to his feelings and emotions in a non-violent way.

- Commitment — Abusers must commit to working on their problem. Without a firm commitment to resolve the problem, they will fall away when the going gets tough. You already know life is tough, and this will test them.

- Motivation — Abusers must be motivated only by their desire to change and improve. One key characteristic of an abuser is that they blame others for their problems. If they are not the sole source of motivation, they will again have a vehicle to continue to blame others as to why they could not complete or change at this time.

- With God all things are possible. They must attend counseling, approved court programs, 12-Step program, or other support group to help the abuser change. It takes hard work to change; much more than "lip service."

Continued on next page

Chapter 10: Types of Abuse, Cycles, Safety, Legal, Continued

Can the abuser change?
(continued)

- Test of time — Abusers must be observed over a long time period to ensure that new behavior patterns have been integrated successfully. The cycle of abuse is clear. There is a honeymoon period where abusers say they are sorry and may try to get counseling and change. Then the daily routines begin and time passes. At some point, tension builds and it is at this point when the abuser and victim must work through this stage with entirely new scripts. This is not an easy task on a good day!

  If the victim accepts them back too soon, they will experience the cycle all over again. Time is the only way to know if that stage can be stopped and corrected.

- Addictions Must Stop — Abusers must stop using any substances that escalate their violence or anger. Alcohol, drugs, gambling, pornography, food or any other vice can easily become a crutch and an excuse for inappropriate behavior. Test their commitment level. If they "can't leave the booze," they will not commit to run the course no matter what they are telling you. Substance use, stress or anger is never an excuse to justify violence or dismiss abuse.

- The abuser must be ready to undergo emotional, physiological and spiritual "surgery." They have to be committed to do whatever it takes to be transformed at every level. If they are not ready to commit to the surgical knife, then they will not change and you should not expect any other outcome. Time to move on!

You may wish to return to the beginning of this Chapter and review the warning signs again. If you feel that you are still afraid or you see behaviors that fit any category, you must take precautions. Do not return to this individual or this situation if you suspect abuse is likely!

God's forgiveness

God forgives those that have hurt us. He models the behavior he expects us to perform.

Continued on next page

Chapter 10: Types of Abuse, Cycles, Safety, Legal, Continued

Can you feel safe and secure back with them

Abusive relationships have three distinct stages and the honeymoon phase is often deceiving. If you are considering getting back together, you need to have had joint and individual counseling. He should be in a program or other men's group to help him connect and hold him accountable for his behavior.

Answer the following questions before considering getting back together. [49]

Does my Abuser:	YES / NO
1. Make me feel safe and secure?	
2. Make me and my loved ones feel threatened, coerced or frightened?	
3. Subject me to violence?	
4. Make me afraid?	
5. Get angry without becoming abusive or violent?	
6. Allow me to freely express my anger, disappointment, frustration or opinion without fear?	
7. Negotiate fairly without accusation and control?	
8. Let me say "No".	
9. Make it clear what he/she is feeling?	
10. Blame me or make me responsible for their anger or frustration?	
11. Respect and allow me to make my own decisions?	
12. Listen to me?	
13. Let me move about freely, go to work or perform errands without permission?	
14. Demand reconciliation based on modifications or concession to behavior? Drop legal charges, wants to move back in the house, threatens financial ruin, or damage to kids..	

Continued on next page

Chapter 10: Types of Abuse, Cycles, Safety, Legal, Continued

Overview

This is just a basic overview of the legal basics. If you have someone who is in need of legal help, refer them to legal counsel. Locate resources in your area and have those ready to provide for women in your group.

Police warning

"Our case was dismissed when the defense lawyer found a loophole in the charges and we left the courtroom. The female police officer pulled me aside and told me that she spent time around my husband during these proceedings and said, 'He is crazy. I've seen too many things like this and I don't want you to end up dead somewhere. Buy a gun and learn how to use it. He just isn't right.'"

Legal

The legal services will vary by area. The State Attorney's Office will have information pertaining to programs for abuser education. Traditionally, these programs are required as part of probation for defendants of domestic abuse cases. As with any course, you get what you want out of it.

If the abuser is ready to change and makes the commitment to do so, these courses will be a refreshing source of information, not just a legal requirement that is a "waste of time." If you are in communication with the abuser, listen to their attitude and description of these courses or programs, which will tell you everything about their desire to change. The programs in your area may be in development; these are similar programs in the USA.

- Domestic Abuse Intervention Program (D.A.I.P.) – This treatment program is for abusers arrested for domestic violence and includes participation in a Domestic Safety Program. [50]

- Domestic Safety Program (D.S.P.) —A six month group counseling and education program for men who batter designed to aide them understand the belief system that supports that behavior. [51]

- Batterer's Intervention and Prevention Program (BIPP)—This program is much more than anger management. BIPP addresses socio-cultural issues, particularly regarding gender and violence, teaches and develops critical thinking skills, and includes therapeutic topic elements such as empathy, accountability, and communication. Often court ordered.

Continued on next page

Chapter 10: Types of Abuse, Cycles, Safety, Legal, Continued

Legal rights   Basic information about legal rights. This information may vary in your area: [52]

- Contact a local shelter or the National Domestic Violence Hotline at 1-800-799-7233 for the most current details, legal updates, available programs, and to find help you need.

- Battery is a crime, regardless of who commits it.

- If you have been assaulted, physically or sexually, by your partner, you are the victim of a crime. You have the right to request an Injunction of Domestic Violence. You may request a Final Protective Order or a Magistrate's Order for Emergency Protection (MOEP). The MOEP is an emergency protective order after an arrest to protect the victim from further abuse or harassment from the abuser.

- If the police are involved and they have probable cause that a battery has occurred, evidence of harm or a witness, they will make an arrest.

- All complaint and arrest affidavits will be reviewed by your legal division.

- Your legal division may have a Victim Witness Assistance Program. This program is designed to help you understand your rights as a victim and can gain access to literature, counseling and other services to assist you during this time whether or not there has been an arrest. They will also support you during the prosecution of your domestic violence case.

- You may contact your local Domestic Violence program direct to access literature, free 9-1-1 cell phones and counseling services or contact the National Domestic Violence Hotline at (800) 799-SAFE.

Continued on next page

Chapter 10: Types of Abuse, Cycles, Safety, Legal, Continued

Family Crisis Centers

Typically in each city, county or district there are government-sponsored programs that are designed to assist victims of domestic violence. Often they have a wide range of services including:

- Basic needs: emergency housing, food, child care, temporary housing, assistance

- Civil legal representation for family, immigration, housing

- Classes/Education: Understanding Abuse, Anger Management, Moving Beyond

- Counseling services

- Crisis intervention

- Employment assistance

- Information and referral

- Law enforcement

- Medical

- Military liaison

- Parenting skills and support

- Prosecution

- Protective orders

- Sexual assault counseling

- Spiritual access

- Substance abuse treatment

Break the cycles

Help you know how to identify abuse, categorize behaviors into types of abuse, recognize the cycle of abuse in your life and seek appropriate help if necessary. In the next Chapter, you will focus on rebuilding your self-esteem and break free of these cycles of abuse in your life.

Continued on next page

Notes:

Section Three Summary

In review

It is your time to throw out the old grounds and start brewing up a fresh cup of java! You are wide awake and Stronger than Espresso.

As a woman you are special, unique and wonderfully made. You have now learned detailed and specific information about the signs of an abuser, types of abuse, safety plans and resources available to assist you.

Actions

Take control:

- Are you clear how you got here in the first place?

- How is your forgiveness for them? For yourself?

- Do you understand the status of your current relationship?

- Did you complete the exercises and assess your level of danger?

- Have you created your safety plan?

- Have you made contact with an outside resource to discuss your current situation?

- Make sure that you educate before you activate so you can remove yourself from the danger zone safely.

- Before accepting the abuser back, make sure to review the Can They Change section.

- Do you fully understand your legal rights?

My VIPs

What were the most Valuable Important Points (VIPs) you learned in this Section:

-

-

-

Continued on next page

Section Three Summary, Continued

Study   Scripture review of the Section. Use this list for further personal study to understand God's word:

Scripture	Objective	Personal Thoughts
1 Peter 2:9	Respect — Self	
Isaiah 1:18	Forgiveness	
Psalms 51:7	Forgiveness	
2 Corinthians 1:3–4	Connections	
Matthew 6:9-13	Forgiveness	
Matthew 5:22–24	Forgiveness	
Matthew 5:44	Forgiveness	
Proverbs 19:11	Forgiveness	
Psalms 103:12	Forgiveness	
1 Corinthians 13:4–8	Spirituality — Love	
John 13:6, 38 John 18: 25-27 John 21:12, 15	Forgiveness	
Psalms 27	Self-esteem — Confidence	
Psalms 28	Self-esteem — Confidence	
Psalms 37	Self-esteem — Confidence	
Psalms 102	Self-esteem — Confidence	

Section 4: Build Your Self-Esteem

Overview

Introduction

The next step to your recovery is to rebuild your self-esteem. Learning what self-esteem is and what causes low self-esteem will help you develop methods to enhance yours. Achieving a healthy level of self-esteem is very important. Understanding the pitfalls you may experience can guard you from setbacks. This is the beginning of a new journey for you and the first day of the rest of your life.

Contents

This section contains the following topics:

Topic	See Page
Chapter 11: Self-esteem Defined	215
Chapter 12: Self-esteem: What erodes? How to enhance?	227
Section Four Summary	246

Objectives

Upon completion of this Section, you will be able to:

- Identify characteristics of low self-esteem.

- Create new strategies to enhance self-esteem.

- Describe how to use scriptures to restore hurts in your life.

- Define causes of low self-esteem.

- Demonstrate the ability to establish boundaries.

Notes:

Chapter 11: Self-esteem Defined

Purpose	The purpose of Chapter 11 is to help you understand what self-esteem is and why it is so important for you to nurture and develop.

I was worthy

"My self-esteem had to be rebuilt so that I could believe that I was worthy of creating a plan of action. The results from the rebuilding process have allowed me to believe in myself and to heal from the pain."

Definition: Self-esteem

Self-esteem is the perception or emotional point of view you have of yourself. It may differ from what could be defined by reason or logic. [53]

What's normal?

After years or a lifetime of abuse, your self-esteem has been bruised. It may feel broken, but now there is hope. It can be restored!

Self-esteem is how you view your value to yourself and to others. It provides a unique picture of how you view yourself at a given point in time. Your self-esteem is as individual as you are and can vary slightly from day-to-day.

Self-esteem can be likened to your coffee order, some days you might want it with one shot, two shots, or a triple shot of espresso. You may prefer non-fat, low-fat or all fat, or you may want your steamed milk light or extra frothy. Your self-esteem can vary depending on your current circumstances, current emotional situation and current relationships.

Self-esteem can be measured as a snapshot where you are right now and can fluctuate. When faced with adversity or a scary situation, it is normal for a healthy self-esteem level to drop; but as the challenge is overcome, it rises.

The foundation for self-esteem begins in the formative years as a child. As you grow older, other influences direct what pathways you cement to form your self-beliefs. Each year, each experience adds more to your self-esteem picture. A person with low self-esteem who is discouraged, weak and inferior is an easy target for abusers. Chronic low self-esteem can be rebuilt.

Continued on next page

Chapter 11: Self-esteem Defined, Continued

Signs of low and high self-esteem

Be encouraged, you have the power to change, enhance and grow your self-esteem the way you want.

What are the signs of each:

Signs of low self-esteem [54]	Signs of high self-esteem
• Overanalyze why you are the way you are.	•
• Fearful and stressed by adversity.	•
• Fearful and worried about the future.	•
• Hopeless.	•
• Unable to set and achieve goals.	•
• Very tired.	•
• Isolate yourself.	•
• Do not make eye contact.	•
• Needy and clingy.	•
• Afraid to take risks.	•
• Negative self-talk.	•
• Do not tell the truth.	•
• Oversensitive to comments from other not intending to hurt you.	•

Recall the age inventory you completed previously in this book? Consider the memories and relationships that impacted your self-esteem development. Describe what your life would look like if that impact dissolved and no longer had a hold on you?

Continued on next page

Chapter 11: Self-esteem Defined, Continued

Historical research on self-esteem

In 1969, Dr. Nathaniel Branden defined self-esteem as, "…the experience of being competent to cope with the basic challenges of life and being worthy of happiness." [55]

Experts disagree over an exact definition; however, Branden's appears to be widely accepted and has withstood the test of time. Branden broadens that definition to include the following primary properties:

1. "Self-esteem as a basic human need…indispensable to normal and healthy self-development."

2. "Self-esteem is a consequence of the sum of the individuals' choices."

3. "Something experienced as a part of, or background to, all of the individual's thoughts, feelings and actions." [56]

Abraham Maslow defined self-esteem to include two kinds of esteem needs, the need for self-respect and the need for respect from others. When these needs are not being met, the individual feels discouraged, inferior and weak. [57]

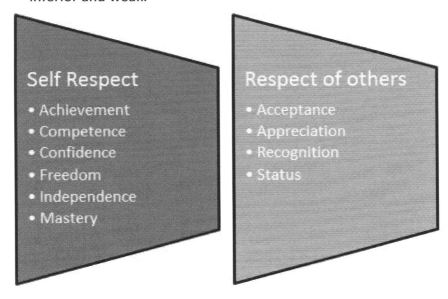

Figure 9. Self-Esteem Needs   Source: Stronger than Espresso, Inc. © 2014.

Continued on next page

Chapter 11: Self-esteem Defined, Continued

Self respect

When you possess self-respect, you have a sense of personal achievement. You believe you are competent and have confidence in your ability to perform daily duties successfully, at home or at work. Will you make mistakes? Of course, but that's all it is. You become free from the ups and downs that pull you from euphoria to despair based on the actions of others. It takes time to master this skill, but it can be yours. God made a promise to you and to us all that he would be our strength, our shelter, our rock.

God's promise to you

Our God is strong and you can have confidence in Him. Part of having a healthy self-esteem is being confident that you can weather the bad times and are still worthy of love and acceptance.

With confidence you are able to "not take it personally" when others are not kind to you or don't act the way you want them to. It is not your fault, nor your responsibility to be in charge of their behavior.

God's promise is that he give us confidence no matter what we face because he is here:

"¹God is our refuge and strength, An ever present help in trouble. ²Therefore we will not fear, Even though the earth be removed, And though the mountains be carried into the midst of the sea; ³ Though its waters roar and be troubled, Though the mountains shake with its swelling."

— Psalms 46:1–3 (NKJV)

"Be still, and know that I am God..."

— Psalms 46:10 (NKJV)

"¹ Hear my prayer, O Lord, And let my cry come to you. ² Do not hide Your face from me in the day of my trouble; Incline Your ear to me; In the day that I call, answer me speedily. "

— Psalms 102: 1–2 (NKJV)

How do you demonstrate you have confidence in God?

Continued on next page

Chapter 11: Self-esteem Defined, Continued

Respect from others

In most cases, abuse victims seek unbalanced approval from others. This need for approval is called codependent behavior. It is a coping mechanism created to survive this relationship, or it has been how you dealt with your immediate family beginning as early as a small child.

You find your value in receiving appreciation from others. You work to please others and become upset or hurt when you do not receive the responses you require. Without their response of love and appreciation, you feel unloved, bewildered and empty.

Freedom comes from knowing that you deserve the respect of others regardless of what you do. You are not responsible for the choices that other people make or the behavior they demonstrate. If they have behavior you do not condone, then it is their choice. God loves you — just as you are. Regardless of how the people closest to you act. His love has no boundaries, judgment or conditions. He is an emotionally safe place for you.

When you respect yourself first, others will respect you. If there are individuals in your life that will not respect you, then they are not a healthy person for you. Creating the distance from those individuals is difficult but it is a part of the process to create personal boundaries.

Describe ways you can expect respect from others.

Continued on next page

Chapter 11: Self-esteem Defined, Continued

Abuser's self-esteem

Having a healthy self-esteem is important.

Self-esteem that is high, but fragile, can be called narcissistic, and it is very common for abusers to have narcissistic traits. With this type of self-esteem, the individual is focused on themselves and display arrogance, conceit and a sense of superiority. However, the display of high self-esteem is not real; it is merely a defensive reaction to their lack of healthy self-esteem.[58] The charade of strong self-esteem can have dangerous outcomes as it is displayed only to fill emptiness inside the abuser versus being soundly based. If their self-esteem is challenged, it can lead to violence.

Self-esteem is the responsibility of the individual, no one else. You are not responsible for their change.

How do you rebuild?

Working toward achieving a healthy level of self-esteem is very important, and understanding the pitfalls you may experience can guard you from setbacks. This is the beginning of a new journey for you and the first day of the rest of your life.

Continued on next page

Chapter 11: Self-esteem Defined, Continued

Self-esteem assessment

Answer the following questions and identify what areas you can focus on to improve self-esteem:

SELF RESPECT	YES / NO
• Do you feel a sense of achievement?	
• Do you feel competent?	
• Do you feel confident?	
• Do you feel free?	
• Do you feel independent?	
• Do you feel you are God's masterpiece?	
RESPECT FROM OTHERS	
• Do you feel acceptance?	
• Do you feel appreciation?	
• Do you feel recognition?	
• Do you feel comfortable with your social circles?	
• Do you feel comfortable telling others No?	

Yes answers are positive and show the areas where your self-esteem is strong.

No answers show the areas you need to focus on:

- Use this information to identify a source of new affirmations. Create new affirmations to say aloud and begin to reprogram.

- Begin to pray that God will help you in a specific area.
  "Search me, O God, and know my heart; Try me, and know my anxieties." **— Psalms 139:23 (NKJV)**

Continued on next page

Chapter 11: Self-esteem Defined, Continued

My self-esteem

How do you know the level of your self-esteem?

There are thousands of tests, books and resources available to check the level of your self-esteem. The fact that you are reading this book shows your eagerness to embrace a new you and improve your self-esteem.

Complete the Self-Esteem Inventory to gauge where you are right now. Be honest and do not think in terms of good or bad.

Review the first column and record how you would currently respond to each situation. Then review the second column outlining what a person with healthy self-esteem person. This gives you a guideline and a goal to work toward as you fabricate and mold the new you. Don't try to perform a tabulation of how you measure up. This is your basis to establish and identify growth opportunities.

"My mealtimes were forgotten because my partner was passed out drunk. Every heirloom I held dear had been smashed during previous fights. Our home consisted of four walls of terror. There was no sanctuary. There was no safe place. I never gave up hope."

Continued on next page

Chapter 11: Self-esteem Defined, Continued

What Do You Do?	Your Typical Response
1. When you make a mistake:	A. Feel ashamed and embarrassed. B. Say you never make mistakes. Fix mistake and hope no one is watching. C. No fear of owning up in public, open to receiving help from others to fix it.
2. When you look in the mirror, what do you see?	Someone who is: A. Attractive and confident. B. An average person and unsure about what to do in life. C. Ugly and insecure.
3. How do you tend to handle a problem:	A. It is never your fault. Blame others. B. Tell others how bad it is but rarely take personal responsibility for the issue. C. Responsible for your actions, thoughts and words. Taking ownership releases you from being a victim.
4. When your wants and needs are different from others you:	A. Give up and give in. Always accommodate others. B. Argue until you get your way. C. Say your needs aren't important. Avoid them altogether. D. Work with others to create a win/win.
5. Your purpose in life is?	A. Feel like you are drifting. Ashamed to admit that you don't know where to start. B. Generally understand what to do and what is capable of creating a life. C. On course with purpose and capable of creating whatever your heart desires.
6. When a comment is made you tend to:	A. Take everything personally and are bruised when anything negative is said. B. Get defensive and respond negatively. C. Value what others say, but know who you are and do not allow others' opinions to change self-worth.
7. Making eye contact is:	A. Easy and effortless. B. Awkward and uncomfortable. C. Extremely difficult and painful.

Continued on next page

Chapter 11: Self-esteem Defined, Continued

Answers:

What Do You Do?	Healthy Self-esteem Responses
1. When you make a mistake?	A. It is normal to not want to make mistakes. Often you feel embarrassed, deny and blame others for your errors. B. Good self-esteem practices allow you to admit your mistakes, take corrective action and learn from them. C. A mistake is only a mistake — no more, no less.
2. When you look in the mirror, what do you see?	Someone who is: A. Our society is focused on beauty and most of us are bombarded with images and messages that you are not good enough. B. When involved in an abusive relationship you can also struggle daily with your self-belief. C. Good self-esteem allows you to accept the things you would like to change without being destructive to ourselves. Self-acceptance of who you are is vital.
3. How do you tend to handle a problem:	A. It is difficult to accept responsibility of our actions. B. Good self-esteem and quality of your well-being is related to the amount of self-responsibility you take. When you blame others you lock yourself into a position of pain. C. When you take ownership for how you respond to what happens to us in life we are free.
4. When your wants and needs are different from others you:	A. Your wants and needs are important. B. Even if others don't respect your needs, you still need to. If you silence your voice, others will not know what you want or need. C&D. Good self-esteem allows you to state your needs, know they are important and learn how to assert yourself. Effective and healthy communication is the key.
5. Your purpose in life is?	A. It is normal to question and wonder what your wish to achieve and what kind of person you want to be. B. Good self-esteem identifies your character and your habits trusting what you really enjoy, what are you good at. Focusing on this information will lead you to be healthier, happier and more successful. C. You have the potential to be more than you might imagine. Remember your life has meaning for you.
6. When a comment is made you tend to:	A. When you become defensive and weigh others' opinions and judgments as more of your own it is difficult to keep perspective. B. Good self-esteem allows you to maintain your strong sense of self-worth regardless of what you hear or others say about you. C. This foundation keeps you from feeling destroyed based on what others say.
7. Making eye contact is:	A. Good self-esteem is supported by direct eye contact. It demonstrates that you are secure and have good self-esteem. B. Eye contact is one of the first impressions others have of you. C. When you feel poorly about yourself you may not feel comfortable making eye contact.

Table 4. Self-Esteem Reponses.

Source: S. Fountain, S. Stephenson, and B. Younglove, *Self-Guided Tour*, National Association for Self-Esteem.[59]

Continued on next page

Chapter 11: Self-esteem Defined, Continued

Restore your self-esteem

Work towards consistent healthy self-esteem practices and refer back to the definitions of healthy self-esteem if necessary. God will help guide you through this discovery process and reveal the next right step. Use this exercise as an opportunity to create new healthy responses. Next you will develop strategies to restore self-esteem.

What Do You Do?	Your New Healthy Self-esteem Responses
1. When you make a mistake?	
2. When you look in the mirror, what do you see?	
3. How do you tend to handle a problem:	
4. When your wants and needs are different from others you:	
5. Your purpose in life is…	
6. When a comment is made you tend to…	
7. Making eye contact is …	

Notes:

Chapter 12: Self-esteem: What erodes? How to enhance?

Purpose

The purpose of Chapter 12 is to identify what erodes your self-esteem and how you can begin to restore yours.

What happened?

Low self-esteem is frequently an outcome of your childhood where abusive patterns began. As you develop strategies to survive, these low self-esteem patterns become your coping mechanisms. As you mature, these patterns can translate to other behaviors that erode self-esteem.

Abusive relationships, depression or other medical condition can also impact and damage your self-esteem.

It is important to remember that despite the external forces that you experience, you are the active participant in developing and maintaining your self-esteem. Your Heavenly Father loves you just as you are! Trust in that fact and take action to improve your self-esteem.

Childhood

Earlier in this book you read the example of two young girls and their shift in self-belief away from 100% perfection as they grew older. Wouldn't it be wonderful to have an answer and to say, it was my parent's fault. Unfortunately, it doesn't work that way. Your parents played a very important role in developing your self-esteem by constructing the basic beliefs of yourself as a child. Often they inserted the "glass ceiling" and named your level of potential as a child. Have you considered if your parents were wrong? God made you as a perfect creation and gave you special gifts. Don't waste it!

- When did you stop dancing and singing like a rock star, and begin critiquing your movements?

- What impact did your upbringing have on the decay of your self-esteem?

- Describe what "glass ceilings" were put on your life?

Continued on next page

Chapter 12: Self-esteem: What erodes? How to enhance?, Continued

What happened?

Action versus blame will help you grow beyond the patterns of the past.

Identifying any glass ceilings or descriptive words from your life can help you understand how you define your potential and purpose.

For example, maybe as a young girl you were told that you could not be anything you wanted to be, but were limited in career choice, intelligence or ability. If your parents told you that you were "stupid," and would never amount to anything, you may have struggled for many years with the burden of disproving that statement. Perhaps you lived up to their limited vision for your life and you have been frustrated and an underachiever all these years.

The best part now is that you are free to believe what you want about yourself! You are not etched in stone and unable to be changed. The messages that you want to change — you can change with dedication and perseverance.

Have no doubt, you have survived an abusive relationship, you are already full of dedication and perseverance and can change anything. You just have to begin. List words to describe you as a child:

Child Descriptive Word	Emotions it Generates

How many of your descriptive words were positive? Negative?

This gives you a foundation to know:

- Emotions that need to be restored

- Memories where you need healing

- People in your life that still have control

- Focus for your prayers for God to transform your self-belief

Continued on next page

Chapter 12: Self-esteem: What erodes? How to enhance?, Continued

Coping patterns

Individuals in abusive situations suffer from low self-esteem. If you were able to bottle self-esteem and drink it up quick, you could finally "get out of this thing" you are in. Since that is not possible, you must slowly begin the process of uncovering where the holes in the self-esteem lie and begin to repair the damage done the hard way.

Each step you take now is one you choose. It is human nature to appreciate more the things that are worked for than those given. Each step you take now will teach you more than you ever imagined. Pray for God to help you, He is there with every step you take.

The important question becomes, why is it okay for him to treat you this way? At some point you must recognize that this is not okay. When you accept that you are not to blame, you release yourself from the belief that you have the power to stop it. While you cannot change your partner's behavior, you **can** decide how to respond to the abuse.

When experiencing low self-esteem often you are emotionally paralyzed and unable to take any action. You become so fearful to challenge your thoughts that you cannot make a change.[60] Even in an unhappy or unhealthy situation, you are safe and secure with the way "it always goes." Instead of risking a new behavior, you maintain the comfort of the past.

Take an example of trying to quit smoking cigarettes or drinking alcohol. Quitting was difficult, the cravings were maddening, but you survived for an entire week and are on the back side. Then...a fight breaks out between you and your husband; you are crying, he screams and storms out and you are left with your broken heart once again. Do you drive to the store to buy cigarettes? Do you pour a glass of wine and suck it down to ease your nerves and calm down? Observe your current pattern of "soothing your child" and begin to think of healthier ways to comfort your fragile ego.

Remember in the definition of self-esteem, when your needs are not being met, you feel discouraged, inferior and weak. These feelings can reinforce your fear and paralyze you so you are not able to make changes. Learn to love yourself and not resort to destructive coping methods.

How do you cope with stress or confrontation?

Continued on next page

Chapter 12: Self-esteem: What erodes? How to enhance?, Continued

Can't break free from the impact of my abusive relationship

A person in an abusive relationship is susceptible to extreme self-esteem damage. To perpetuate the Cycle of Violence, the abuser gives approval during the honeymoon period to give hope that the situation will improve. When the victim relies on the abuser to give them "pats on the back," then the ability to crash occurs when the approval is withdrawn. When the tension builds and violence erupts, the victim's self-esteem is decimated and plummets. The victim's only hope is that during the next honeymoon cycle they receive the positive strokes they need from the abuser to rebuild their self-esteem.

Recognize that as long as you remain in the abusive situation, it will be extremely difficult, if not impossible, to repair the damage done. The inability to remove yourself from hurtful people and hurtful words does not allow you the peacefulness you need to clear your mind and begin living in a new way. The chances to build a foundation for healthy self-esteem, and maintain a consistent balance are greatly impaired, if not impossible in an abusive setting.

Medical concerns

Many people have low self-esteem because of a medical condition. Low self-esteem caused by a medical condition is different than trauma because the medical condition may require continued treatment to keep it under control. Individuals who experience anxiety, depression, phobias, post-traumatic stress disorder or have an illness and/or disability can have a negative self-image. [61]

If your low self-esteem is caused by a more serious illness, and you do not identify it, you can work all you want on your self-esteem and still remain defeated.

It would be like treating a rash with topical cream only, when you really need to stop eating the food you are allergic to. It is not your fault and you have done nothing wrong if you find yourself with this diagnosis.

Seek the help of a medical doctor to discuss your situation and treatment options that are best for your needs.

Continued on next page

Chapter 12: Self-esteem: What erodes? How to enhance?, Continued

Action inventory

As long as we hold onto the past, we cannot grab onto the future. God has blessings in store for you. In that you can trust. Taking actions every day you can begin to restore your self-esteem.

What are ways that we can begin to restore our self-esteem?

Major Hurt / Memory	Person (s) Involved	Your Feelings?	Action(s) You Will Take Today to Overcome

Continued on next page

Chapter 12: Self-esteem: What erodes? How to enhance?, Continued

Good does exist

Don't forget the good that has happened in your life. The GOOD in your life is very important to focus on! Reflect on WHY it was good, and the feelings you experienced then and now as you remember.

To remember and replace is an action. Action requires work, but it is worth it.

- Let it go = release resentment (for you!)

- Forgiveness = freedom (for you!)

- Stop believing = no more lies (for you)!

Describe the memories, people or events that helped you feel good about yourself.

What pieces of those memories can you use to apply to actions to overcome?

Continued on next page

Chapter 12: Self-esteem: What erodes? How to enhance?, Continued

Time to enhance

After spending time identifying what erodes self-esteem, now you are ready to begin to learn new ways to enhance your self-esteem.

Loving God is your first right step

You can be assured that the first step to improving your self-esteem is to accept God's love for you. There is no one else in this world like you. You are unique and wonderfully made.

You can have confidence that He will make a way for you.

"However, it is written; 'no eye has seen, no ear has heard, no mind has conceived what God has prepared for those who love him.'"

—1 Corinthians 2:9 (NIV)

I love my....

Loving yourself can be hard work sometimes.

Write 5 things that you absolutely love about yourself:

1. I love my _____.

2. I love my _____.

3. I love my _____.

4. I love my _____.

5. I love my _____.

Describe what challenges you had finding five things you love about you?

It is unfortunate, but many women struggle to think of even one item that they like or even love about themselves. If you got five, hats off to you.

If you weren't able to complete all five, come back to this later. Your goal is to be able to rattle off five things you love about yourself. Then ten great things about you, then 100 awesome things about you!

Love yourself, like God loves you.

Continued on next page

Chapter 12: Self-esteem: What erodes? How to enhance?, Continued

How to enhance self-esteem?

There are many ways that you can enhance self-esteem and thousands of good sources of information for ideas. You can go to the local bookstore, library and internet and find ideas for ways to enhance your self-esteem. There is a wealth of resources at your fingertips ready to be drunk up by you.

Many advise to make mealtime special, display your personal belongings, or make your home a sanctuary. All of these are wonderful ideas, but may not be available to you right now. When reviewing methods to enhance self-esteem and you are currently in an abusive relationship, you may not have the freedom to try a number of these tips.

There are self-esteem changes that you can put into place in your heart and mind at the beginning. As you grow away from this relationship, you will be able to feel comfortable in your own skin. Slowly you will be able to expand to include all of the tips that are made available to you. Do what you can now and grow taking baby steps toward your goals.

What are you doing now to feel good about yourself?

Identify God's blessing over your life

Reviewing God's word is the best way to start your restoration. Understanding what he has in store for you and the blessings he has granted over your life can help. Taking verses and discovering their application to your life is where God can transform your life through the Bible.

Read **Psalms 103:1–6**

Continued on next page

Chapter 12: Self-esteem: What erodes? How to enhance?, Continued

Verse	Psalms 103:1-6 (NKJV)	
1	*"Bless the Lord...and all that is within me."*	What blessings has God given you?
2	*"...Forget not all His benefits."*	Describe the benefits to accepting the Lord's blessings?
3	*"Who forgives...who heals."*	What iniquities need forgiving in your life? What diseases of yours need healing?
4	*"Who redeems your life...Who crowns you with loving kindness..."*	What does loving kindness and tender mercy look like?
5	*"...our youth is renewed like the eagles."*	If you could soar like an eagle, where would you go?
6	*"...justice for all who are oppressed."*	In what areas do you want justice?

Continued on next page

Chapter 12: Self-esteem: What erodes? How to enhance?, Continued

Affirmations and self-talk

In Chapter 7 you identified the key changes you were going to make to your inner music.

How has your self-talk changed since you began this process?

Change the voices in your head from positive versus negative. Each day speak affirmations to reprogram your self-talk. Write in a journal. Keep a small notepad in your purse and begin to make notes as to what you say to yourself so you can begin to track your inner music.

If the thoughts are negative, rewrite the negative into positive statements and begin reprogramming your mind to believe that you are beautiful, fabulous, gorgeous, smart, and strong.

You might be saying things like, *"I am so stupid." "Why am I so fat?" "I never do anything right."*

If you struggle with loving yourself, just begin your new self-talk to say, "God loves me just as I am," which releases His blessings over you and releases you from the destructive influence of your damaging words.

Continued on next page

Chapter 12: Self-esteem: What erodes? How to enhance?, Continued

Appreciation

Appreciate all the good things in your life right now. Celebrate your life as it exists now, not only the life you dream about. Even if everything is at the lowest point, you are still alive and were wonderfully made by your Creator. Your life, in whatever state it currently exists, is the fingerprint of God. Keep hope, keep faith and keep your eyes focused on your goals.

"Rest in the Lord, and wait patiently for Him; Do not fret..."
— Psalms 37:7 (NKJV)

Thank God for 10 things in your life:

1.

2.

3.

4.

5.

6.

7.

8.

9.

10.

Continued on next page

Chapter 12: Self-esteem: What erodes? How to enhance?, Continued

Associations

Associate with people that have a positive outlook on life and different interests than what you have been doing in the past. Even if new people seem dorky, strange or weird, it is good to branch out and make new associations at this time. Places to find new groups: public library, local state park nature course, church, local community charity or clean-up day, and other volunteer efforts. Stay clear of "singles" groups at this time as you are developing a love affair with your new self, not another partner.

Scripture tells us that it is important for us to select our associates carefully:

"[7] You used to walk in these ways, in the life you once lived. [8]But now you must rid yourselves of all such things as these: anger, rage, malice, slander, and filthy language from your lips. [9] Do not lie to each other, since you have taken off your old self with its practices and have put on the new self, which is being renewed in knowledge in the image of its Creator."

— **Colossians 3:7–9 *(NIV)***

"Do not give what is holy to the dogs; nor cast your pearls before swine, lest they trample them under their feet, and turn and tear you in pieces."

— **Matthew 7:6**

Get moving

Take a few minutes every day and move your body.

Whether you just put on the radio and stretch your muscles, dance around the house as you do laundry, or head out the door for a walk around the block, just begin to move your body and learn how it feels to be free.

Do not critique your style or your moves; learn about what feels good to you. You can bike, jog, run, walk, or anything else you can imagine. Start your body to build inner strength and self-confidence.

Prayer walking is another great way to spend time walking in your neighborhood or in a park and you pray for the homes you pass or people that go by.

Continued on next page

Chapter 12: Self-esteem: What erodes? How to enhance?, Continued

Food

You've heard it before, eat your vegetables, drink plenty of water, and don't eat too many sweets.

Guess what...it is true. Healthy food decisions show self-respect and can make you feel better.

Select five to six servings of fruits and vegetables, six servings of whole grain foods like bread, pasta, cereal and rice, and two servings of protein foods, such as beef, chicken, fish, cottage cheese, yogurt or cheese. If you are vegetarian or vegan include protein rich grains such as barley or quinoa and include legumes or soybeans to your diet. Ensuring that you receive complementary amino acids, Vitamin D and other nutrients.

Make these food choices healthy and stay away from junk food. Removing junk food removes sugar, salt and fat from your diet. You can eat three square meals a day or numerous smaller meals, whatever is best for your system.

The goal is to offer a diet that provides the fuel you need to heal emotionally, and restore your body ravaged by years of unhealthy and toxic environments. The best part, you might even lose a few pounds of fat or find it easier to build muscle tone too!

Connect

Finding that you are not alone and sharing your concerns can validate your feelings. When your emotions are validated, you can begin healing and this will boost your self-esteem.

*"Though one may be overpowered, two can defend themselves. A **cord** of **three** strands is not quickly broken."*

— **Ecclesiastes 4:12 (NIV)**

Don't go it alone. Join a Stronger than Espresso® connect group, mentoring or coaching program. If you have joined, we welcome you to our STE Sisterhood.

What are ways you can connect with others?

Continued on next page

Chapter 12: Self-esteem: What erodes? How to enhance?, Continued

Be still

Learning to be still and have quiet time can be very difficult. God reminds us throughout the Bible to, *"...be still and know I am God."* —Psalms 46:10

You have grown accustomed to "walking on egg shells." You may be accustomed to consistently looking over your shoulder, sleeping with one eye open, or even shielded others from erupting violence. Learning to have quiet time can be challenging.

Take heart that in time it will get easier. In the beginning you may experience panic, nausea, difficulty concentrating, changes in breathing and other "fight or flight" responses. There are ways to help you learn how to quiet your mind in conjunction with other soothing activities. Be mindful to focus on only the calming activity.

Some other ideas:

- Take a bubble bath. Keep the room silent, no phone, TV or radio, to experience quiet serenity. Focus on the water comforting your skin, and how you can release tensions away with your breath. Take caution to ensure you feel safe with doors locked before you begin.

- Brew a cup of tea. Focus on the entire process of heating the water, watching it steep, and drinking it, say nothing and do nothing else. Enjoy being in the moment. This is not a time to also sort the daily mail while the water heats up. Concentrate on only the tea.

- Pray daily. Spend time with God asking him to reveal items you need to know. This is an active time to seek God.

- Meditate. This is a quiet time. Many people pray during this time also. In the beginning it can feel like a curse to be left alone with your own thoughts. It is common to have difficulty lying quietly. You can focus on the in and out rhythm of your breath or repeat one affirmation to keep your mental "noise" at bay. As you mature this quiet time will become easier and you can focus on one thought.

- Phone a friend. Connecting with others is important for healing.

- If you are a mom, model how to ask and set healthy boundaries. Using clear communication and respect is an important lesson to demonstrate to your kids.

- Invite someone to talk a walk. Fresh air can do wonders.

Continued on next page

Chapter 12: Self-esteem: What erodes? How to enhance?, Continued

**Personal
Hygiene**

Make sure to groom, dress and take care of yourself each day. Keep your hair and nails neat and clean.

Check your insurance coverage to see if preventative care visits are covered. Check for and schedule any well-woman examinations, that are due, such as pap exam, mammogram or routine blood work to verify health.

Check a local thrift store, church or women's shelter for low cost or free clothing to bring a new item to your wardrobe. Creating these habits will teach you how to respect yourself and help others respect you.

Reading

What you read can transform your spirit.

"²² The lamp of the body is the eye. If therefore your eye is good, your whole body will be full of light. ²³ But if your eye is bad, your whole body will be full of darkness. If therefore the light that is in you is darkness, how great is that darkness!"

— Matthew 6: 22, 23 (NKJV)

Read the Bible book of Psalms. Psalms is an inspirational book written in song and prayer. David's life was very much like our own: troubled, full of ups and downs, and numerous occasions where he cried out to God for help. There is betrayal, celebration, lamenting, trials and tribulations.

Psalms Chapters 35, 36, 37 and 91 are great places to start when you feel emotionally attacked.

As you begin the process of building your self-esteem, make sure to search your local library, book store and internet for information. You will find enormous resources available that are wonderful and free for you to access. Small changes that you make each day will begin to build the stepping stones you need for your new walk in life.

Continued on next page

Chapter 12: Self-esteem: What erodes? How to enhance?, Continued

Remove toxins

Remove toxins from your life. Remember Chapter 6 on Coping Behaviors? You may have discovered that you do not make good coping choices. Is yours use of physical toxics: alcohol, cigarettes, illegal drugs, prescription drugs, overeating excessive? Do you choose avoidance, isolation, or unhealthy relationships?

Each of us will identify different items that need to change. Toxins, in whatever form they are, will cloud your recovery and continue to perpetuate your situation. You may disagree, and say, "I am finally free of the abusive relationship. I want to be free and do whatever I want." It is vital that you begin to clean your body, mind and soul to free you from the grip of vices. This is the beginning of respecting yourself. Let God's love and his word show you how to live your new life. Give yourself approval to spend time on you!

Stop procrastinating

Our pain makes us immobile at times. When you stop working to please others there can be an "uncomfortable" transition. You are not as "busy" as before spending all your time pleasing everyone. Your pendulum can slow to a new tempo.

This change in tempo can leave some voids. You have not been given the pleasure of working on items or projects that you would like to enjoy or do.

Make a list of simple projects that you have been putting off. Try to complete them over time to feel a personal sense of accomplishment.

Trust your inner self

God gave your body and mind the capability to be full of wisdom. Learning to trust your inner voice is the beginning step to self-respect. If your body needs sleep, rest. If your body needs sustenance, eat. If you feel lonely, take time to call on a trusted friend for companionship. If you feel drawn to a specific place or heard repeated comments of the same item, take notice. If your gut feels something, listen. Following these notions teaches you to listen to yourself and respect the inner knowledge you already have.

Continued on next page

Chapter 12: Self-esteem: What erodes? How to enhance?, Continued

Write it down

Write down your feelings, notes, comments and observations. You can journal or make a brief account of what transpired for the day. Just be consistent so your feelings release instead of churning internally. When you reflect on your emotions, you will be surprised at the progress you have made.

When you pray, have a notebook close by so you can record the messages, impressions or emotions that God reveals to you in that quiet time.

Natural talents

What are you good at? Are you good at: listening, gardening, or organizing things? Whatever your talents are write them out, review them and be proud. These are your God-given talents, find opportunities to incorporate them into your week's activities.

What you like to do

Write out 10 things you like to do. They may overlap the list of things you are naturally good at and that is okay. It can be as simple as swinging in a playground, but if you like to do it, it counts. Review the list and look for similarities. Try to accomplish an item per week until completed.

Tests and trials

When you begin this journey, it will be exciting at first, but there will come a time when you will be tested. Don't expect that this will be a walk in the park. The tests will come and be difficult. Keep focused and if you get off track, don't be ashamed, just try again. God will be with you. He forgives you. Just get back up, ask for help, and try again.

Habits

You will be tempted to fall back into your old habits. Your old coping behaviors may be overwhelming at times. Resist this urge and continue to focus on your new path. Make a list of your old habits and what new behavior you will do instead. Be proactive, look for answers when you are clear headed, not angry or upset. Phone a friend and ask for help or to talk you through it. Isolation is a dangerous place on this road of your restoration.

Continued on next page

Chapter 12: Self-esteem: What erodes? How to enhance?, Continued

Mind games

Be watchful for other peoples' opinions and the mind games that the abuser will play. You have been manipulated for a long time and you are not changing anyone else, just you. Do not communicate with your abuser if possible, so that you can remain free and clear of the mind and word games. Stay focused and trust your inner wisdom. Check with neutral parties, contact a women's advocate or women's shelter to discuss what is happening between you and the abuser.

Painful journey

Commit to run the course. This journey will be painful, but well worth the challenges you endure. Do not be discouraged, continue to persevere.

Self-talk

Listen and change your self-talk. Be mindful that you must work hard to make this change. If you allow the old voice to continue to break you down, you will take two steps forward and one back.

Support

Having support during this time is very important. Often you will turn inward because you have been doing that for so many years. Avoiding support at this time can stagnate healing. You need to make sure that you focus on individual activities that promote healing and self-respect, and pair them with group activities and counseling. As a victim of abuse, you have been isolated in many ways and you need to learn to reach out, communicate and trust other people again. This allows you to restore who you are and rebuild new relationships.

Continued on next page

Chapter 12: Self-esteem: What erodes? How to enhance?, Continued

Fear

Remember, while in or under the fear of an abusive relationship, the crawl to healthy self-esteem can seem unattainable. It can feel like you are sitting on a three-legged stool, and every time you get just about there, a leg gets kicked out from underneath you. You can work on your self-esteem, but you will be continually bombarded by influences that distract you or make you feel you can't do this. Recognize that this will happen. Believe it will not be forever. Trust that you can do this and anything you wish.

Release your fears and your worries to God and focus on your healing. Your self-esteem is your responsibility and building it can be done. Believe in yourself and begin trying today. With persistence and a personal commitment, you will be transformed.

God is not fear. When you feel fear, anxiety or worry, you can be assured it is not of Him. His Word reminds us to not be afraid.

"Don't worry about anything; instead, pray about everything. Tell God what you need, and thank him for all he has done. If you do this you will experience God's peace, which is far more wonderful than the human mind can understand. His peace will guard your hearts and minds as you live in Christ Jesus."

— Philippians 4:6–7 (NLT)

Describe things you are afraid of; or worry about?

You can always say, *"God did not give me a spirit of fear, but of love, power and a sound mind!"* **2 Tim 1:7.** God I give these fears to you. I trust you!

You can improve your self-esteem. It will require patience and dedication in order to restore. There is hope!

"It has been almost a decade since I was subjected to an abusive relationship, but those years of conditioning have stayed with me. Low self-esteem, fear and anxiety continue to cloud how I perceive myself and my environment."

Section Four Summary

In review

Working to maintain a healthy level of self-esteem is vital for our self-confidence needed to take on new projects, manage interpersonal relationships and accept new challenges and risks for personal growth. Although self-esteem may vary slightly from day-to-day, your foundation can be fortified so regardless of any storm, no future erosion occurs.

In an abusive relationship, the management, control and care of your self-esteem is often given away to the abuser. Take back control of your own self-esteem. You are responsible for the level and well-being of your self-esteem.

Actions

- Honor self-respect and demand respect from others.

- Review the self-esteem inventory to maintain a target of the person you wish to be.

- Set self-esteem goals and write out steps to meet your goals.

- Recognize the warning signs of low self-esteem. If you notice a tendency to gravitate to these beliefs or feelings, take evasive action. If you have medical problems that exacerbate low self-esteem, such as depression, seek professional help to teach you how to move beyond that phase of your life.

- Love yourself.

- Identify your best methods to enhance your self-esteem. Put those habits into practice daily.

- Know your pitfalls. Admit mistakes. Let go of shame. Get back on track.

- Release fear — it is not of God.

- Recognize this is the first step of many to a life-long transformation. Set aside time for daily discussions with God. Spending time with Him will help you believe you are God's masterpiece.

Continued on next page

Section Four Summary, Continued

My VIPs   What were the most Valuable Important Points (VIPs) you learned in this Section:

-
-
-

Study   Scripture review of the Section. Use this list for further personal study to understand God's word:

Scripture	Objective	Personal Thoughts
Psalms 46:1–3	Self-esteem — Confidence	
Psalms 46:10	Self-esteem — Confidence	
Psalms 102:1–2	Self-esteem — Confidence	
Psalms 139:23	Self-esteem — Confidence	
Psalms 103:1–6	Forgiveness — Grow beyond	
1 Corinthians 2:9	Self-esteem — Confidence	
Psalms 37:7	Blessing	
Colossians 1:7–9	Patience	
Matthew 7:6	Connect	
Ecclesiastes 4:12	Self-esteem — Confidence Connect	
Matthew 6:22, 23	Knowledge — Wisdom	
Philippians 4:6, 7	Self-esteem — Confidence	

Notes:

Section 5: Redefine Your Life

Overview

Introduction

You've made it to the last Section! This is when you take all that you have learned and put it in to action. You will create an action plan and begin your journey for the rest of your life renewed, strong, and powerful. Embracing God as you have you will never be alone whatever joys or trials you face.

Contents

This section contains the following topics:

Topic	See Page
Chapter 13: Seven Ingredients to Perfection, #1 God, and #2 Body	251
Chapter 14: Seven Ingredients of Perfection, #3 Soul, and #4 Mind	275
Chapter 15:Seven Ingredients, #5 Words, #6 Lessons, and #7 Relationships	295
Section Five Summary	313

Objectives

Upon completion of the Section you will be able to:

- Demonstrate the ability to apply the seven measures of perfection to your lives.

- Identify the Seven Ingredients of Power: Your God, Your Body, Your Soul, Your Mind, Your Words, Your Lessons and Your Relationships.

- Describe how they will use the power of God to sustain your transformation.

- Identify changes to make in your life to protect your body and mind from future abusers.

- Describe how the lessons of the past can reshape the future.

- Communicate the ways you will connect with others.

Notes:

Chapter 13: Seven Ingredients to Perfection, #1 God, #2 Body

Jolt awake	Time to crank up the espresso machine and serve triple shot power! You are ready to Jolt Awake in life.
Purpose	The purpose of Chapter 13 is to accept God's amazing love and grace in your life. When you hold this power at the center of your being, you can live in freedom.
Redefine your life	By accepting God's amazing love and grace in your life, you hold the power to your future and to live in freedom. When you climb a tree feed with living water your experience transforms from the natural to the supernatural.
	This book has focused on identifying your patterns of behavior, understanding your abusive relationships, and steps to building self-esteem.
	What's the next step?
	Now you are ready to create your plan of action and get your life in motion. This Chapter helps you create your seven measures of perfection. By blending all seven ingredients you will craft a new you to last a lifetime.
You are a survivor	Congratulations, you are ready to take the first step to define the new you as a strong survivor capable of boundless miracles.
	You are a **survivor** of domestic violence! Do not use the word "victim" when you describe yourself anymore. That is the past; you are ready for your future.

Continued on next page

Chapter 13: Seven Ingredients to Perfection, #1 God, #2 Body, Continued

Focus on you

The next step in your recovery is to begin to focus on you — not the abuser. Fill your ears, mouth, and mind with your name, not the abuser's name. Over the past months, years and for some decades, your focus has been on meeting the needs of an abusive partner. In doing so, your needs were not met or discussed. It is time to stop talking about the abuser.

You may have spent hours talking to friends, coworkers, counselors, police, and perhaps been required to testify in court. You have relived the trauma over and over again. Make a tick mark on a piece of paper each time you speak their name or when you update others about the abuser's tactics. You will be surprised how many times per day your thoughts and words turn to them.

Sharing your story and asking for support from those around us is vital at first, but you can experience diminishing returns. Some people relish in the mire of your drama. They may unknowingly continue to "stir the pot" and find excitement in getting all the up-to-date gossip about your life. Look at our television line-up of reality shows and you can see that curiosity is a basic human trait. This behavior can perpetuate your victim persona, keeping one foot rooted in the past. Staying stuck in the past can damage your self-confidence and restrict your jump to the next step.

Reach out and connect with Christian women in the church, women Pastors, or Pastor's wives to get the help you need.

Your story has power to heal others

Behind every story is a survivor. You have a powerful testimony to share.

You had the worst boss in the world. You could do anything — had to do everything. You have handled intense pressure, and simultaneously protected others around you. You endured unbearable situations and still rose from the ashes. Yes you are Stronger than Espresso!

"And they overcame him because of the blood of the Lamb and because of the word of their testimony, and they did not love their life even when faced with death."

— Revelations 12:11 (NIV)

Continued on next page

Chapter 13: Seven Ingredients to Perfection, #1 God, #2 Body, Continued

Coffee is power As you come to the most active part of the Stronger than Espresso® journey, you need to understand the keys ingredients to perfection:

Key Ingredient	Power that makes it possible
1. Someone created the coffee plant and designed the beans to be produced for consumption.	God
2. Physical components that are required: body, water, coffee pot.	Body
3. Passion to brew a perfect cup of java.	Soul
4. Must possess the mental know how to mix each ingredient.	Mind
5. Use as a tool for conversation with others and part of a daily habits.	Words
6. Experience on how to brew, what portions and how you like it to taste.	Lessons
7. Who you share it with and an opportunity to meet with others.	Relationships

Continued on next page

Chapter 13: Seven Ingredients to Perfection, #1 God, #2 Body, Continued

Your seven key ingredients

Seven Ingredients of Perfection are what you need to restore your life. Each ingredient is required for you to restore and transform.

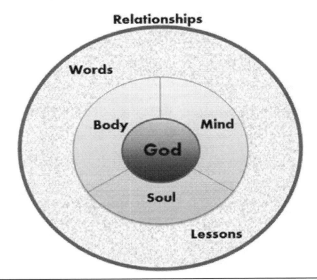

Figure 10. **Seven Ingredients of Perfection** Source: Stronger than Espresso, Inc. © 2014.

1. Ingredient #1, Power of God — Giving power to your God, faith as a tool for survival, setting new standards for self.

2. Ingredient #2, Power of Your Body — What to wear spiritually, healthy eating, healthy practices, managing trauma symptoms.

3. Ingredient #3, Power of Your Soul — Assertiveness, boundaries, healthy relationships.

4. Ingredient #4, Power of Your Mind — What you believe is your reality.

5. Ingredient #5, Power of Your Words — Internal and external speech.

6. Ingredient #6, Power of Your Lessons — What you have learned and what is yet to learn.

7. Ingredient #7, Power of Your Relationships — How bringing healthy people into your life can reconnect you to a lifelong change.

Continued on next page

Chapter 13: Seven Ingredients to Perfection, #1 God, #2 Body, Continued

**Power of God
Ingredient #1**

The #1 Ingredient to the Seven Measures of Perfection is the **Power of God.** It is amazing, awesome and incredible. Faith is the belief in the existence or knowledge in someone or in something you accept as truth.

You don't see gravity, but you have faith if you drop something it will fall to the ground. You don't see oxygen molecules, but you have faith that they are present and they will keep you alive when you breathe. As a babe you relied on your parents to teach you what they knew, and had faith that what they taught you was true.

**Our God is
strong**

Having spiritual faith gives you the support to rely on and security that you are loved. This confidence guides you through this journey to survive your situation. Through faith you can have hope that you will grow beyond this pain and be made whole again.

Looking upward instead of inward allows you to focus on a greater power.

Throughout this book we have shared numerous scriptures from the Bible that describe God's strength for us in times of trouble.

"For in the time of trouble He shall hide me in His pavilion; In the secret place of His tabernacle He shall hide me; He shall set me high upon a rock."
— Psalms 27:5 (NKJV)

"23The steps of a good man are ordered by the Lord, And He delights in his way. 24Though he fall he shall not be utterly cast down; For the Lord upholds him with His hand."
— Psalms 37:23,24 (NKJV)

"The Lord is my strength and my shield; My heart trusted in Him, and I am helped; Therefore my heart greatly rejoices, And with my song I will praise Him."
— Psalms 28:7 (NKJV)

"I am holding you by your right hand – I, the Lord your God. And I say to you, 'Do not be afraid. I am here to help you...'"
— Isaiah 42:13 (NLT)

Which scripture is your favorite? Why?

Continued on next page

Chapter 13: Seven Ingredients to Perfection, #1 God, #2 Body, Continued

A measure of faith

When making a journey of healing, working on your spiritual self is a priority. Having faith plays a vital role in establishing hope and increasing the chances of human survival.

At Stronger than Espresso® we believe that Jesus Christ is our Savior and the way to eternal life. Accepting him into your heart will bring blessings into your life and the Holy Spirit will transform your life. This does not mean you will not face difficult times or hardships, but you will never again do it alone.

Regardless of your particular religion or spiritual beliefs, faith is a common theme in theology. The word "faith" or concept of faith is described in most of the major religions of the world today.

This concept, though widely debated as to its exact definition, existence and validity, weaves its description through the major religions of the world. If you were to ask anyone who has been "touched by faith," they will most undoubtedly tell you that their lives have been blessed and they could not consider their existence without their faith.

Everyone has a measure of faith. At times in our lives we desire spiritual pathways even if we don't know why or exactly what we are looking for. This is your measure of faith yearning to be filled with God's great love. In order for God to lead your life, you have to accept Him in your life.

"For I say, through the grace given to me, to everyone who is among you, not to think of himself more highly than he ought to think, but to think soberly, as God has dealt to each one a measure of faith."

— Romans 12:3 (NKJV)

Continued on next page

Chapter 13: Seven Ingredients to Perfection, #1 God, #2 Body, Continued

Tried it all

"I tried everything alcohol, drugs, exercise, journaling, angel cards, praying, daily journals, mediation, yoga, reading spiritual books by the dozen and even took a trip to China to touch the largest Buddhist statue in the world to fill this desire. I finally accepted Jesus into my heart. It was awkward at first but over the years I have been amazed by the blessings he has put into my new life, my new family, my new spiritual growth beyond my dreams. Now I can't imagine my life without Christ at the core."

God never stops loving you

God's love is unbelievable! He loves you just as you are. He loves you for what you have been, all that you are and all that you will be, regardless of the decisions or events you have made.

When you are able to embrace yourself and love yourself like God loves you, an amazing transformation occurs and you are energized with the power of faith!

"I was also blameless before Him, And I kept myself from my iniquity."

— Psalms 18:23 (NLT)

"I knew you before I formed you in your mother's womb. Before you were born I set you apart and appointed you as my prophet to the nations."

— Jeremiah 1:5 (NLT)

"Not even a sparrow, worth only half a penny, can fall to the ground without your Father knowing it. And the very hairs on your head are all numbered. So don't be afraid; you are more valuable to him than a whole flock of sparrows."

— Matthew 10:29 (NLT)

"Long ago, even before he made the world, God loved us and chose us in Christ to be holy and without fault in his eyes."

— Ephesians 1: 4 (NLT)

Which scripture is your favorite? Why?

Continued on next page

Chapter 13: Seven Ingredients to Perfection, #1 God, #2 Body, Continued

Release your burdens

Our burdens can feel so heavy. We carry them around unaware that God's promise is He will carry those burdens for us. All we have to do is give them away.

Describe the burdens you are carrying right now?

When you awaken the spiritual part of you there is a transformation that occurs. When you "give it to God" you are released from the burden you carry around. By trusting in God you set aside fear. Grab hold of the hand of the Almighty and follow the pathway of joy, understanding and freedom.

"...How can you say the Lord does not see your troubles? He never grows faint or weary. No one can measure the depths of his understanding. He gives power to those who are tired and worn out; he offers strength to the weak. Even youths will become exhausted, and young men will give up. But those who wait on the Lord will find new strength. They will fly high on the wings like eagles. They will run and not grow weary. They will walk and not faint."

— Isaiah 40:27-31 (NLT)

"The Lord is my shepherd; I have everything I need. He lets me rest in green meadows; he leads me beside peaceful streams. He renews my strength. He guides me along right paths, bringing honor to his name. Even when I walk through the dark valley of death, I will not be afraid, for you are close beside me. Your rod and your staff protect and comfort me. You prepare a feast for me in the presence of my enemies. You welcome me as a guest, anointing my head with oil. My cup overflows with blessings. Surely your goodness and unfailing love will pursue me all the days of my life, and I will live in the house of the Lord forever."
— Psalms 23 (NLT)

Continued on next page

Chapter 13: Seven Ingredients to Perfection, #1 God, #2 Body, Continued

---

Release your burdens (continued)

"I look up to the mountains — does my help come from there? My help comes from the Lord, who made the heavens and the earth! He will not let you stumble and fall; the one who watches over you will not sleep. Indeed, he watches over Israel never tires and never sleeps. The Lord himself watches over you! The Lord stands beside you as your protective shade. The sun will not hurt you by day, not the moon at night. The Lord keeps you from all evil and preserves your life. The Lord keeps watch over you as you come and go, both now and forever."
                                                    — Psalms 121:1–8 (NLT)

"The Lord is close to all who call on him, yes, to all who call on him sincerely."   **— Psalms 145:18 (NLT)**

"Then Jesus said, 'Come to me, all of you who are weary and carry heavy burdens, and I will give you rest. Take my yoke upon you. Let me teach you, because I am humble and gentle, and you will find rest for your souls. For my yoke fits perfectly, and the burden I give you is light."
                                                    — Matthew 11:28–30 (NLT)

"Don't put your confidence in powerful people; there is no help for you there. When their breathing stops, they return to the earth, and in a moment all their plans come to an end. But happy are those who have the God of Israel as their helper, whose hope is in the Lord their God. He is the one who made heaven and earth, the sea, and everything in them. He is the one who keeps every promise forever, who gives justice to the oppressed and food to the hungry. The Lord frees the prisoners. The Lord opens the eyes of the blind. The Lord lifts the burdens of those bent beneath their loads. The Lord loves the righteous. The Lord protects the foreigners among us. He cares for the orphans and widows, but he frustrates the plans of the wicked. The Lord will reign forever. O Jerusalem, your God is King in every generation! Praise the Lord."
                                                    — Psalms 146:3–10 (NLT)

Continued on next page

Chapter 13: Seven Ingredients to Perfection, #1 God, #2 Body, Continued

**Release your
burdens
(continued)**

1. Of the six scriptures you just reviewed, which scripture did you connect with the most and why?

2. What burdens will you give to God right now?

3. What are the consequences if you do not let Him take over your burdens?

Continued on next page

Chapter 13: Seven Ingredients to Perfection, #1 God, #2 Body, Continued

Security

When you believe that you are a beautiful child of God, you begin a spiritual path that will heighten your self-worth.

You are loved no matter what you do.

With this security of love:

- You form a new basis of internal strength and allow you to set new standards.
- Treat yourself with self-respect.
- Quiet the negative messages you have been receiving internally and externally.
- Respect yourself by making appropriate decisions about your well-being.
- Make better food choices.
- Make better choices of moral content.
- Trust your inner voice and spiritual wisdom.

"[35] Can anything ever separate us from Christ's love? Does it mean he no longer loves us if we have trouble or calamity, or are persecuted, or are hungry or cold or in danger or threatened with death? [36] (As the Scriptures say, 'For your sake we are killed every day we are being slaughtered like sheep.') [37] No, despite all these things, overwhelming victory is ours through Christ, who loved us. [38] And I am convinced that nothing can ever separate us from his love. Neither death nor life, neither angels nor demons, neither our fears for today nor our worries about tomorrow – not even the powers of hell can separate us from God's love. [39] No power in the sky above or in the earth below – indeed, nothing in all creation will ever be able to separate us from the love of God that is revealed in Christ Jesus our Lord."

— Romans 8:35–39 (NLT)

Continued on next page

Chapter 13: Seven Ingredients to Perfection, #1 God, #2 Body, Continued

Glorious shifts

Awakening your faith and spiritual self will begin a shift in your moral guidelines.

Reading **Matthew Chapters 5–8** will help give you an understanding of the basic life lesson Jesus teaches. "Treat others as you wish you to be treated" and "love your neighbor as yourself" are simple and basic. If you are to love your neighbor as yourself, but don't love yourself how can you do this.

Proverbs also has guidelines for healthy Godly living. There are 31 books so just reading one chapter a day during the month can support your changes.

Your moral compass will naturally shift due to the influence of the Holy Spirit. You will begin respecting your body as a temple. When you do this, you begin to eat and drink appropriately to surround yourself with people which will fill holes in your heart. These "cravings" for food, alcohol and sex are replaced with God's limitless love and no longer drive your behavior and coping mechanism.

As you spend more time with God, what shifts have you noticed in your life?

Continued on next page

Chapter 13: Seven Ingredients to Perfection, #1 God, #2 Body, Continued

How to pray

Prayer is very personal and is different for everyone. There is no wrong way to pray, but sometimes people are confused as how to pray.

There may be days when all you can do is pray and ask, "Show me how I can survive today." You may cry out to God and ask, "Why?" in anguish and pain. When you are on the brink and cry out to God, you create music to His ears.

Your life was never created to be easy. It is the challenges and lessons you sustain that make it worthwhile. You may rejoice when you feel his presence wrap you up and you begin to see light at the end of a very long, dark tunnel. In almost every circumstance, expect the valley before the joy on the mountaintop can be enjoyed.

When you are afraid, remember, that you will never be alone. God's love does not leave you and is always there for you all you have to do is reach out and ask for it. Have faith and ask for guidance, love and support.

A few prayer tips:

- Pray often and plan to spend time with God daily. This allows you to have more time to "hear" Him through the power of the Holy Spirit.

- Thank God for the blessings in your life. God never wastes a hurt so your hardship could be a blessing in disguise.

- God will hear your prayers.
  "Now this is the confidence that we have in Him, that if we ask anything according to His will, He hears us."
  — 1 John 5:14 (NKJV)

- God operates in his own time. Patience is a key to wait for answered prayer.
  "Rest in the Lord, and wait patiently for Him; Do not fret…"
  — Psalms 37:7 (NKJV)

Continued on next page

Chapter 13: Seven Ingredients to Perfection, #1 God, #2 Body, Continued

---

How to pray
(continued)

- Pray with other Christians:

"19Again I say to you that if two of you agree on earth concerning anything that they ask, it will be done for them by My Father in heaven. 20 For when two or three are gathered together in My name, I am there in the midst of them."

— **Matthew 18:19–20 (NKJV)**

"Pray over him, anointing him with oil in the name of the Lord...pray for one another, that you may be healed."

— **James 5:13–16 (NKJV)**

"Pray for us; for we are confident that we have a good conscience, in all things desiring to live honorably."

— **Hebrews 13:18 (NKJV)**

Action

Complete the following questions:

- Define the Power of God in your life?

- What changes are you going to ask Him to make?

- What burdens will He take over today for you?

- With those burdens gone, what will you now be free to accomplish?

Chapter 13: Seven Ingredients to Perfection, #1 God, #2 Body, Continued

Power of Your Body Ingredient #2

Your body is the temple to your soul. The #2 Ingredient to the Seven Ingredients of Perfection is the **Power of Your Body.** It is the vessel of strength that allows you to experience this wonderful life you have been given. You will create rules of respect and a treatment plan for your body.

You are already beautiful just as you are. This isn't a quick-fix program to make you okay by shedding a quick 20 pounds or making you more beautiful overnight. Rather this is about creating self-love, self-respect and a new definition of who you are. When you have been denied focusing on yourself for so many years, or thought it selfish to do so, this freedom will be foreign and uncomfortable. Being a self-respecting individual is much more desirable than a martyr. It will take time and dedication, but well worth it.

Continued on next page

Chapter 13: Seven Ingredients to Perfection, #1 God, #2 Body, Continued

What to wear

One of the first things we worry about when we wake up is what we are going to wear today.

Have you ever considered what God's word says about what you should wear?

"[12]Therefore, as the elect of God, holy and beloved, put on tender mercies, kindness, humility, meekness, longsuffering; [13] bearing with one another, and forgiving one another, if anyone has a complaint against another; even as Christ forgave you, so you also must do. [14] But above all these things put on love, which is the bond of perfection."

— Colossians 3:12–14 (NKJV)

"[14]Stand therefore, having girded your waist with truth, having put on the breastplate of righteousness, [15] and having shod your feet with the preparation of the gospel of peace; [16] above all, taking the shield of faith with which you will be able to quench all the fiery darts of the wicked one. [17]And take the helmet of salvation, and the sword of the Spirit, which is the word of God."

— Ephesians 6:14–17 (NKJV)

"It is God who arms me with strength and makes my way perfect."

— Psalms 18:32 (NKJV)

"[12] The night is far spent, the day is at hand. Therefore, let us cast off works of darkness, and let us put on the armor of light...[14] put on the Lord Jesus Christ...."

— Romans 13:12, 14 (NKJV)

"She is clothed with strength and dignity, and she laughs without fear of the future."

— Proverbs 31:25 (NKJV)

- Describe new items that you will wear?

- What are the benefits to include these in your wardrobe?

Continued on next page

Chapter 13: Seven Ingredients to Perfection, #1 God, #2 Body, Continued

5 senses	One easy way to begin to change your body is to start by indulging your five senses: What are the five senses?

Sight	Begin to change what you see around you:

- Place a few items of importance around your home that makes you feel good. This can be: throw pillows, knick knacks, plants, family photographs, awards or affirmations by the light switch in each room. Think about what makes you feel happy and secure, and add that to your home.

- Find a piece or two of clothing that makes you feel good about yourself and add to your wardrobe. If you are on a budget, thrift stores can be an excellent and economical source, or a women's shelter may have a "dress for success" outreach program.

- Seek out a spiritual place for you. Be still in the moment when you are there. Look around you, feel how your body calms.

- Stare at something you enjoy: the neighbor's flower garden, the rain pattering on the window, clouds floating through the sky, a kite at the park, or your dog sleeping.

- Go for a walk in your neighborhood and spend time seeing all of the interesting creations that surround you. The roly-poly bug on the ground, the clutter of junk on your neighbor's porch, the twisted vine branch that looks like it will come to life if you stare at it long enough. Begin to be aware of your environment and surroundings.

- Go to a new place. If you always go to a local tavern, change to a local library or the botanic gardens and wander through the flower park.

What are things you like to see or places you would like to go?

Continued on next page

Chapter 13: Seven Ingredients to Perfection, #1 God, #2 Body, Continued

Sounds

Select sounds around you that are uplifting and refreshing:

- Listen to music you like.

- Sing out loud and praise your voice even if it's off key.

- Turn off the television. Try to read or just be quiet. This can be most difficult at first with all your racing thoughts – stay the course, it is well worth it. Having no sound can be very healing. Turn off the television at night when you sleep. Many people swear they cannot sleep without the television on, yet most of them suffer from insomnia as a general rule. The television noise from shows and commercials try to get your attention. When you are asleep, these loud sounds can wake you and disrupt sleep. Silence can be hard at first, but you will learn that it is golden to healing.

- Try to stay away from anyone who yells, uses foul language or is negative in their speech. If your brother-in-law always screams at your sister; your neighbor complains about her life; your work friends run down the job and other people; then remove this negativity around you. Focus on enrichment and enlightenment. Protect your time and who you choose to be around you.

- Surround yourself with positive words. Attend a service of a progressive church and hear upbeat music and an uplifting sermon free of condemnation. Try a Stronger than Espresso® class. Go to a local library and check out books on tape to fill your car with positive words each day versus the noise of commercial radio. Talk to people who are happy and positive about life.

- Find new sounds that you like: such as, birds outside your window, the sound of your child's voice, your heartbeat and the simple act of listening to your own breath. Listen to your voice when you sing a particular tune and you may realize you really can sing after all. You might also find that having no sound and quiet moments will bring you the most comfort at this time. Try both.

Continued on next page

Chapter 13: Seven Ingredients to Perfection, #1 God, #2 Body, Continued

"As I began to heal, the strangest thing happened. I must have been releasing toxins from bad choices, hurts and deep emotional pain that had been stored in my cells, muscles and organs. As I healed, my joints ached and for weeks I had a cough that tasted like anesthesia flavor. As I spent time daily in prayer, I would ask God to cleanse my body of this toxicity. It was similar coughing out a mist. It was my body healing. This lasted for weeks and then it stopped. God confirmed that he needed room for his Holy Spirit to work in my life and I was too full of the past for him to move freely in my soul."

Taste

Your mouth should enjoy what you bring into your body for nourishment:

- Drink plenty of water. Add lemon to make increase the detoxification ability, add a small amount of fresh vitamin C to your diet and make the water more pH balanced. Be careful to not drink just bottled or purified water because during processing it is stripped of precious minerals. Filtering tap water allows you better taste and retains water's natural minerals.

  When under extreme stress and trauma, the body can hold tension in the muscles and in the cells. As you begin to renew your life, cleansing each part of the physical body is very important. Water provides oxygen to the cells and is vital for life removing body toxins out of the body. Use this simple but life sustaining liquid to the fullest. When you drink a glass of water be mindful and say positive affirmations to yourself as you drink. "I cleanse my body now and am restored and refreshed."

- Make sure to eat healthy meals every day. When experiencing a stressful situation, sometimes you do not remember the last time you ate. Stop abusing your body this way. Decide on three healthy meals per day or perhaps six smaller meals each day and stick to that program.

- Enjoy going to the grocery store again and notice the varieties of unique fruits and vegetables, legumes, whole grains, breads, meats and other products you may have never noticed before.

Continued on next page

Chapter 13: Seven Ingredients to Perfection, #1 God, #2 Body, Continued

Taste
(continued)

- Hold off on the fatty, processed foods, chips, cookies and candy; it will make you feel worse. If you are overwhelmed emotionally, an easy healthy sandwich with whole wheat bread, lettuce and tomato, meat and cheese can be a complete meal with little exertion. Just remember to eat good food. Fuel your brain and fortify your body, the temple, with strength. This alone is an act of self-respect.

- Caffeine - Be mindful of your caffeine intake. Too much caffeine can elevate heart rate, upset stomach, irritate bowels, and create feelings of anxiety or panic attacks. Coffee, iced tea, cola and diet cola, chocolate, and some pain medications all have caffeine. With increased intake your resistance to caffeine builds up and then you require higher levels to give you the boost you need. Caffeine is addictive and there are withdrawal symptoms; the most common is a severe headache. There is much controversy on the amount of caffeine that is acceptable. Many say that no more than 400 – 450 mg per day and, for nursing or pregnant woman the limit is 150 mg – 300 mg per day. It varies, but an 8 oz. cup of coffee has on average 100-110 mg of caffeine. Note that most standard coffee mugs hold closer to 12 oz. of liquid so you need to measure to know your actual intake. You are best to learn how your body is affected by caffeine, and if you are experiencing anxiety symptoms; less is better. Tea, on the other hand, has about one-third the caffeine per cup. Depending on the tea, the caffeine can be even less. When looking at options to reduce caffeine evaluate all of the beverages, food and supplements you are taking to check for caffeine intake.

Continued on next page

Chapter 13: Seven Ingredients to Perfection, #1 God, #2 Body, Continued

Taste
(continued)

Remove the toxins —This has been preached throughout this book and is vital to your recovery process!

- Smoking – If you smoke, understand why you smoke. Often this behavior learned in your youth and is associated with rebellion and escape from tension. That is why so many people can quit in the beginning, but relapse when the tension of life occurs. Try to quit. It will give you confidence, save you money, make you smell better and best of all it releases you from the bonds of your past!

- Alcohol – Stop drinking for a period of time. Later on you can reintroduce alcohol socially or for special occasions. For now, get to know a sober you. You will save money, protect yourself from new violations of your mind and body, cure a "poochy" tummy and will release you from "clinging to that friend in the bottle." When you do not drink alcohol, your mind remains clear and you can see things for what they are. Remember, victims of abusive relationships have a very strong tendency to find comfort through alcohol. You do not want to fall into that trap. You must learn a new way to live and survive in the moment, rather than escaping your troubles with alcohol.

- Drugs — Illegal or legal/prescription drugs can be a problem. If you are doing illegal drugs, please quit and find a new method of comfort. There are local centers that can help you with any drug problem you need assistance with; just ask. Doctors can also prescribe prescription drugs which can be highly beneficial as part of a trauma treatment program or pain management program. However, their usage should be short lived as they become like candy to your soul. You are trying to create new coping skills, and while drugs can be vital to your success in the beginning, you must learn to trust yourself to be competent on your own.

What are your favorite tastes?

Continued on next page

Chapter 13: Seven Ingredients to Perfection, #1 God, #2 Body, Continued

Touch

Human's desire touch, you need it to exist. Don't deny yourself. Touch can come in many healthy ways. Hugs are a great place to start if you are comfortable with that. Right now stay focused on healthy touch versus romantic touch found in one night stands or quick relationships. Right now all your energy should focus on your healing. You are vulnerable to be influenced, exploited or used by others.

- Write something. Take the time to write in a journal, write a poem, write affirmations, write how wonderful you are, write your observations to the exercises in this book, and write a friend a letter.

- Enjoy the pleasures of a hot, bubble bath on your skin. Let the water and scented suds envelope your skin and soak away tension and worry.

- Play with your children or with your pet. Hug, love and laugh your cares away. Go to a pet store and touch the kittens or puppies.

- Hug someone you love and trust. When you have shut yourself down emotionally you can become distant to others. This protection mechanism is very important, but human touch can be very healing, if given by an appropriate party, in a non-sexual way. If you do not like to be hugged right now, understand that is okay too.

- Create something. Whether you paint, glue, tape, bake, or build you can be very satisfied making something new. Don't judge yourself harshly. Who cares if it's ugly or not a masterpiece, you made it and at best, can get a giggle out of your own creation. Creating something allows you to work in the right side of your brain. Often when doing this, you lose track of time as your thoughts are free of the time — keeping left brain. This freedom is important to stimulate your imagination. Learning how to access your full brain power is important to healing and will promote self-confidence.

Continued on next page

Chapter 13: Seven Ingredients to Perfection, #1 God, #2 Body, Continued

Touch
(continued)

- Wear a piece of clothing or scarf that feels great to you. Maybe it is an angora sweater, silk blouse or a suede vest. Pick something that feels lovely against your skin and that you love to touch.

- If you are single, abstaining from touch of a sexual nature at this time can be of value while you are healing. There is no denying that it can feel great to be loved and to have the attention of a new lover. You may not want to believe it, but you are very vulnerable right now and sexual behavior can begin an entirely new set of events and circumstances that you are not yet ready for. There is so much self work to be done and you need to finish what you have begun first. Only then can you to determine what type of partner you seek. You need to spend time educating and preparing for the next stage so you will not make the same mistakes again. There will always be time for love — later.

What are changes you can make for the touch points in your life?

Smell

Your nose can guide you:

- Fill your home with scents that you enjoy, that might be fresh flowers, air freshener or a specific air spray.

- Note smells around you and see what memories they stir up. Often a scent reminds us of a memory. When they arise you can deal with the emotions that it stirs in a healthy fashion and then release the memory. No more stuffing it down deep again.

- Clean out animal areas that could be bringing a foul odor to your home. This is not healthy for you or your family.

- Be aware of smells that you do not like or seem out of place. If you have a foul or smell that is out-of-place you may search and find no danger. One example from a survivor is they would smell the scent of a candle that had just been blown out; but there is no candle lit. This scent would at times surround them. Sometimes strange unexplained smells occur and they are more supernatural than natural. If you feel that is the case, pray and ask God for understanding.

Continued on next page

Chapter 13: Seven Ingredients to Perfection, #1 God, #2 Body, Continued

**Power of Body
Action plan**

In order to make changes you first need to identify actions you can take to make changes you desire in your life.

Complete the chart for all five senses. List specific items that you will do for yourself for each sense. Include simple and everyday changes you can begin to make immediately. Once those items become habit, revisit this exercise and include more.

Sense	I want to change... *(identify)*	To change I will start... *(action)*	I commit to this change for... *(time)*
Sight			
Sound			
Smell			
Taste			
Touch			

Chapter 14: Seven Ingredients of Perfection, #3 Soul, #4 Mind

Purpose	The purpose of Chapter 14 is to help you create goals and redefine your vision and purpose in your life. These actions glorify God and His purpose for your life. Reestablish the importance to keep your mind full of positive thoughts. If you think a thing, it can become a thing. Knowing your thoughts impact the ultimate outcomes.
Power of Your Soul Ingredient #3	The #3 Ingredient to the Seven Ingredients of Perfection is the **Power of Your Soul.** Your soul is a gift from God. It is unique. There has never been, nor never will be another soul like yours. Your soul should have the freedom to be all God created you to be.
Definition: Gyroscope	"A gyroscope is an apparatus consisting of a rotating wheel so mounted that its axis can turn freely in certain or all directions, and capable of maintaining the same absolute direction in space in spite of movements of the mountings and surrounding parts." [62]
Create Your Personal Gyroscope	What you need now is to define your personal gyroscope.
	This device, once spinning, tends to resist changes to its orientation. Life happens and you will be thrown curve balls. Learn to have the self-confidence to allow you the ability to resist being thrown off course. Define your personal orientation, how to maintain it and how to resist changes to its orientation. When creating your personal gyroscope it is easier to do with the help of a girlfriend.
Girl to Girl Rules	The next few pages will contain information that you can receive from a good girlfriend. Honest feedback to help you get better and get on with your life!

Continued on next page

Chapter 14: Seven Ingredients of Perfection, #3 Soul, #4 Mind, Continued

Girl to Girl
Rule #1

Focus on your dreams, spiritual gifting and what you like to do!

Get to know yourself. It is time for you to accumulate all of the information that you have gleaned from this book and begin to generate a plan of action. Any good plan states a goal and the baby steps required to meet that goal.

Focus on your dreams:

- Pretend that you are approaching your 80th birthday and write yourself a letter.

  Be specific to communicate what things are important. Make sure to speak to what dreams you wish to have accomplished. Let your older and wiser self communicate to you now about what dreams are hiding inside you.

- Make a list of your dreams. You have been setting aside your dreams because of someone else, or perhaps told that, "oh, you're dreaming, that will never happen." Remember the scripture from **Matthew 19:26 (NKJV)**, "...with God all things are possible" and you can attain any dream that you want.

  Before a dream can be achieved it must be allowed to be created and formulate. Take time now and make a list of any dream, idea, desire, want or fantasy that you can think of. Don't censor yourself; just write what comes to mind no matter how foolish or ludicrous.

  I dream of...

Continued on next page

Chapter 14: Seven Ingredients of Perfection, #3 Soul, #4 Mind, Continued

Girl to Girl Rule #1 (continued)

Discover the moments when you are the most fulfilled. Max Lucado, in his book, *Cure for the Common Life, Living in your Sweet Spot,* describes an exercise that you search for the moments in your life that you were the most at ease, the most comfortable, the most happy. These moments, Lucado calls the "Yes" moments and how you know that you were made to do that.

It could be when you are baking bread at Christmas, when you developed a complicated spreadsheet for your homeowners' board meeting, played a competitive tennis match or a walk in the woods.

You are wonderfully made and our Creator has given you a special set of traits and characteristics, unique to only you.

These are the actions, activities and skills that you do effortlessly. Search your past and make a list of these moments, describe what you were doing and why you felt so happy. You will begin to see correlations to these memories that can lead you to understand what special strengths you possess. [63]

Describe your gifts:

-
-
-
-
-

"There are different kinds of spiritual gifts, but the same Spirit is the source of them all." **—1 Corinthians 12:1-12 (NLT)**

"Do not neglect the gift that is in you, which was given to you by prophecy..." **—1 Timothy 4:14 (NKJV)**

Select future pursuits that include these natural strengths allow you to feel complete and whole.

Continued on next page

Chapter 14: Seven Ingredients of Perfection, #3 Soul, #4 Mind, Continued

**Girl to Girl
Rule #1
(continued)**

Spending time on getting to know you is the best foundation you can set for your future:

- Describe what action frees you to "play"?

- Describe your favorite daily habits or rituals.

Understanding your habits and desires can help you begin to live more comfortably as the new you. Each of you has different ways to learn or complete tasks. There are many correct ways to achieve the same objective.

Imagine the simple task of tying your shoes. Some people make two loops and then tie them together, others make one loop, circle and slip through. Both ways are correct, but a different method to achieve the same goal. By describing the habits you like, allow you to respect a part of you and incorporate it into your daily lifestyle.

It is also easier to communicate to others your preferences when you have identified them for yourself. For success in a future relationship, it is important for you to establish an individual style now. You will be able to communicate your preferences so they can choose to conform to your needs as much as you will to meet their needs.

- List a consistent group of people in your life that have been stable and loved you unconditionally. What traits do these people share?

If you want this list of people to grow, start to include in your daily affirmations or prayers that this group is being formed - even now for you to access.

Continued on next page

Chapter 14: Seven Ingredients of Perfection, #3 Soul, #4 Mind, Continued

Girl to Girl Rule #1 (continued)

- Being alone is not the same as being lonely. Part of the trick when you break off any relationship is to learn to be alone with yourself.

  When you are quiet, what sounds do you hear? Do you hear the whispers of God? Do you hear how bad you are? Do you fill your room with noise of TV, radio, friends? Do you drink alcohol to excess? Are you uncomfortable that you have no one to blame anymore?

  Describe all of the emotions or fears that you are experiencing right now or are afraid of.

Girl to Girl Rule #2

Set Your Goals.

Keep your heading by setting your goals and displaying them prominently. You need a constant reminder of what is important and where you are going.

Goal setting is a fantastic way to direct your gyroscope and set new headings. It lets you take baby steps on the daily level, yet shows the path where you are headed. Without goals, you can find yourself a year or two later feeling discouraged because you have not accomplished what you wanted.

If you want in one year to take a trip abroad, then you must make saving money for the trip now a daily or weekly goal. If you want to learn the language before the trip, then you would need to include a language course or foreign language program as part of your steps too.

Tips to set goals:

- Write out what you want and note the individual steps necessary to work toward the goal.
- Goals are personal. They are yours and not set for others.
- Make them realistic. You want to succeed.
- Don't over commit. You can always add to your goals later.
- Give them a timeframe: short-term, mid-term, long-term.
- Once goals are achieved, create new ones.
- Review them often to check progress or adjust as needed.

Continued on next page

Chapter 14: Seven Ingredients of Perfection, #3 Soul, #4 Mind, Continued

**Girl to Girl
Rule #2
(continued)**

Discover areas that you want to grow or change. This will give you the foundation to set your initial goals:

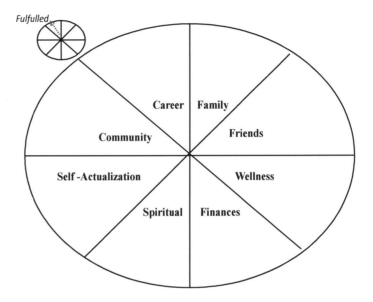

Figure 11. Goal Discovery Tool.   Stronger than Espresso, Inc. © 2014.

1. For each of the eight sections, make a pinpoint mark in the pie based on how fulfilled you feel in that area. If you are very fulfilled in that area, make your mark in the outer area of the pie. If you do not feel fulfilled in any area, make your mark inside the pie near the center.

2. Once done making eight separate dots, connect all the dots with a line. It will look like funky spider legs. You will see which sections you need to work on to become more fulfilled.

3. On the sections that you are not as fulfilled, pause and reflect on how you feel about yourself when you read the topic heading.

4. Create specific goals for those specific areas.

5. Describe any emotions, memories or thoughts that surface.

Continued on next page

Chapter 14: Seven Ingredients of Perfection, #3 Soul, #4 Mind, Continued

**Girl to Girl
Rule #2
(continued)**

Begin by setting daily goals that are reasonable and attainable.

Take baby steps and allow yourself success.

Keep the goal list displayed as a constant reminder.

Make sure your goals are: specific, measurable, attainable. Goals should be time specific. Common goal timeframes are:

Short-term	Mid-term	Long-term
Daily	90-day	5 years
Weekly	6 months	10 years
Monthly	1 year	Beyond

Once you meet a goal, replace it with a new one. That is how you begin to live a life of growth and development.

As you rewrite your goal list, keep previous lists in a file folder so you can refer back. It is fun several years from now to go back and see what your goals were, the ones you have successfully completed, and others that were replaced with new ones as your life matured.

Write your goals:

Short term —

Mid-term —

Long-term —

Continued on next page

Chapter 14: Seven Ingredients of Perfection, #3 Soul, #4 Mind, Continued

**Girl to Girl
Rule #3**

Take Care of Your Emotional Health.

Making a list of personal rules is important for your emotional health.

Sample Rules for Emotional Health: [64]

- I will take care of myself. I will take time to rest, eat well, exercise and spend time with people who I like doing the things I want to do.

- I will find the positive in my life experience instead of focusing on the negative.

- I will let go of my past.

- I will respect myself and take responsibility for my actions.

- I will acknowledge and take credit for successes and accomplishments.

- I will make time to develop one or two close relationships where I can be honest about my thoughts and feelings.

- I will talk positive to myself.

- I will remove myself from hurtful or damaging situations.

- I will accept that life is about choices and always brings change.

- I will have plan for my future.

Make your list of your new personal rules:

-

-

-

-

-

Copy this list and post in a visible location so that you will see it often and reinforce your new personal rules.

Continued on next page

Chapter 14: Seven Ingredients of Perfection, #3 Soul, #4 Mind, Continued

**Girl to Girl
Rule #4**

You must learn how to trust God, yourself and others.

You must build the ability to trust your inner self and know that you contain all the pieces of the most beautiful story; the puzzle of your life. This includes paying attention to your needs and wants and knowing when a person or situation is bad for you. By developing this inner trust, you will be able to discern and decide more appropriate behaviors to act upon.

There are physical responses you have to other human beings. Have you ever been around someone who gives you the creeps or gives you bad vibes? Your body is full of eternal wisdom at a cellular level. You experience physical characteristics when someone bad for you is nearby. Your body may react and feel tense, your heart race, throat tighten, jaw clench, hold breathe, or your stomach and intestines may tighten. Your acuteness to hear your body communicating can be deadened if you are filling your body with garbage: noise, bad food, alcohol, cigarettes, stress, or suffer from sleep deprivation.

Earlier in the book was the statement, "When it feels good for you — do it. When it does not feel good — do not do it." God made your body to work to communicate in a way so you can listen for messages and trust your inner wisdom. Know when something feels good or not to you before saying yes.

- Describe times that you listened to that inner voice or moved away from a situation or person and later found that you were spared from harm.

- How did that message come to you and how did you feel?

- What were the circumstances that kept you from following your inner wisdom? You did not listen to that wisdom and later said, *"I knew better." "I knew I shouldn't have done that?"*

- Describe what it feels like when you know someone is bad for you. What physical symptoms do you experience?

Continued on next page

Chapter 14: Seven Ingredients of Perfection, #3 Soul, #4 Mind, Continued

External trust

After being hurt for many years in an abusive relationship, you often believe that you will never trust anyone again. Learning that you can trust a family member or a friend to truly love and accept you just the way you are is vital to your healing journey.

Trust in others for a support system is very different then the trust level required establishing a new romance. At this time, it is strongly recommended that you wait until you complete the work on yourself first before attempting a romantic endeavor. If you pursue a relationship, know that trust must be earned over time.

In God we trust

Once you let go and let God rule your thoughts, emotions, choices and actions, your life can really begin to grow.

"[5] Trust in the Lord with all your heart, And lean not on your own understanding; [6] In all your ways acknowledge Him, And He shall direct your paths." **—Proverbs 3:5,6 (NKJV)**

Trust is earned

Trust is earned. You cannot live your life constantly questioning and not believing in others. You are not required to trust someone just because they are a nice person. Trust will be earned by others in a slow and methodical fashion.

Here is an example about trust You ask a neighbor to watch your children for two hours while you attend a class. You ask her to show up at 6:30 p.m. If she is on time — trust is earned. However, if she is late, offering excuses, which in turn forces you to be late — she will not have earned your trust. You will think twice before letting her handle things important to you.

Another example is you tell a friend private information and ask her to keep it confidential. The next day you hear your information from a third party. The friend did not earn your trust.

Developing relationships with others builds your support system again. The fact is that you must learn to trust again in order to heal. This time, you have the right to make small opportunities for others to earn your trust and be selective on whom you invite into your trusted circle.

Continued on next page

Chapter 14: Seven Ingredients of Perfection, #3 Soul, #4 Mind, Continued

**Girl to Girl
Rule #5**

You are responsible for your own actions and behaviors.

As part of your healing journey, you will need to learn how to be personally responsible for your actions. The only person you can affect any change in is you. Determine how you want to be, set a course and go for your goals.

It is much easier to live to please yourself than be a skittish young child trying to be a chameleon blending in seeking love and approval. When you live to please yourself first, you will find that you stop being anxious, sleepless or having racing thoughts.

At first, when you begin making this transformation, you may feel agitated, awkward or bored because you are not accustomed to looking inward. You are so used to running and fixing things for others that you have spent so much energy to that goal.

When you stop going around pleasing people, you free yourself from that unattainable goal. This behavior is also called being codependent and is a coping mechanism that you developed over your lifetime. You can be free!

What things in your life do you need to let go of because it is not your burden anymore?

List steps you can take to make a change in that area.

Continued on next page

Chapter 14: Seven Ingredients of Perfection, #3 Soul, #4 Mind, Continued

**Girl to Girl
Rule #6**

Don't sweat the relapse. Regroup and try again.

What if you start to slip back into you old habits?

It will happen that you will begin to slip into some old habits. This may cause you to be frustrated or ashamed.

There are several things to consider should you begin to slip back to old behaviors:

- Know yourself. You already know what you do when things go bad. You might run, get angry, drink, clean, or isolate yourself. Whatever it is, this is your coping mechanism.

  Describe a list of your coping mechanisms, and think of ways you can retool them when an incident occurs.

Coping Mechanisms	New Behavior

- Be honest— Lying could become a coping mechanism and a method of survival for you. You have lied to yourself saying things would get better. You probably lied to friends or family about the severity of your abuse so they would not meddle and make things worse. You lied at work because you didn't want to be turned down for the promotion because of trouble at home. You lied to those critical of you because you stayed.

- This circle of lies kept you trapped. Without the truth, you may become dizzy and so mixed up that you had trouble finding your way out. If you hear yourself lying now, even small white lies, recognize that you may be slipping into old patterns.

Continued on next page

Chapter 14: Seven Ingredients of Perfection, #3 Soul, #4 Mind, Continued

**Girl to Girl
Rule #6
(continued)**

- Addictive behaviors surface. Survivors of trauma often turn to substances to receive relief from their suffering. Should you find yourself turning to alcohol, food, gambling, prescription or illegal drugs or other vices be quick to pull yourself back. Do not feel shamed if you fall down. Pick yourself up, dust off and get back on your road to recovery.

- Selecting new abusive or unsupportive relationships. Be quick to recognize the people around you and make changes to those relationships if you feel they are abusive or unsupportive. The longer you wait the higher the risk you will begin to slip further into this pattern. Ask the opinion of the few trusted individuals you have close to you, and listen to their wisdom. If they have a bad feeling about someone, do not be blinded by the excitement of a new relationship, be honest with your own instincts and open to the wisdom of friends and family.

- Self destructive behaviors. If you begin to speak destructively to yourself, to not eat properly, or to not take care of yourself, then action should be taken immediately. Seek help from your therapist, a support group or seek out self-help material on how to turn this behavior around. Be honest about your behavior, do not beat yourself up and wallow in your failure. Make efforts to get back on the right path and try to articulate why you fell back.

Understand this journey is not a straight line. You are crawling from the valley to the mountain and it will not be easy. You can release yourself from shame when you are honest about where you are in your healing process. If you make a mistake, correct it and move on, always keep your eyes on your goals.

Continued on next page

Chapter 14: Seven Ingredients of Perfection, #3 Soul, #4 Mind, Continued

Girl to Girl
Rule #7

Don't Go it Alone.

Let Friends, Family and Support Networks Know They Can Help!

Much of your emotional growth will be done internally, but it is vital that you build your own support system. Begin to surround yourself with people that you can trust. You should look for new friends that have the habits and values of people you <u>want</u> to have. Start learning something new and it will expose you to new people with a common interest. Join the Stronger than Espresso® connect groups. Go to a local library for a class or join a church for fellowship and activities. Enjoy meeting new people and be mindful of your inner wisdom on how you feel around these new people and situations.

Often, people will ask what they can do to help. At this time they will often come forward telling you what they really felt about the abuser confirming that there was something wrong. They may feel guilty that they didn't help you earlier. Sometimes our friends and family can have the best intentions, but they can exacerbate the problem because they force you to keep reliving your saga and do not allow you to move on.

Friends and family may want to help, but may be at a loss as to how to help you as you heal. If asked, share these tips with them.

How to help a loved one that has experienced trauma? [65]

- Ask — Ask if help is needed for mundane tasks, errands or just to lend a hand.

- Empower — Aide in establishing routines to bring life back into control.

- Listen — When ready, let the survivor talk about the experience to acknowledge, validate and reduce isolation.

- Reassure — Affirm you are not to blame for abuse and are not alone.

- Research – Offer help finding answers and resources.

- Support with patience — There is not pre-determined healing timeline.

Continued on next page

Chapter 14: Seven Ingredients of Perfection, #3 Soul, #4 Mind, Continued

Girl to Girl Tips   A summary of the girl to girl tips:

1. Focus on your dreams, spiritual gifting and what you like to do!

2. Set your goals.

3. Take care of your emotional health.

4. You must learn how to trust God, yourself and others.

5. You are responsible for your own actions and behaviors.

6. Don't sweat the relapse. Regroup and try again.

7. Don't go it alone. Let friends, family and support networks help!

Continued on next page

Chapter 14: Seven Ingredients of Perfection, #3 Soul, #4 Mind, Continued

Power of Your Mind Ingredient #4

The #4 Ingredient to the Seven Measures of Perfection is the **Power of Your Mind.** If you think a "thing," it can become a "thing." Break the negative reoccurring statements over your life and replace them with positive and productive affirmations, prayers and blessings over your life.

How our thoughts shape our reality

The power of your mind is extraordinary, and can create your reality. If you believe something then it can be true. If you believe certain limits about yourself, this can restrict your options or reality. Pay special attention your thoughts and the outcomes they can create. Your thoughts can make the difference between success and failure.

For centuries people believed that the world was flat and that you would fall off the edge should you try to sail too far. It was only those that would take risks and tempt the danger that man was able to grow beyond their present status. In history there are examples of the power of the mind. From professional athletes, cancer survivors, prisoners of war, or victims of abuse, despite the difference of the circumstances, in all cases the will to survive was formed in the mind first.

Goal check-back

Creating our goals is the first challenge. The next hurdle is to incorporate our written goals into measurable daily choices. Only when changes to our choices are made, can our lives move in a new direction.

Describe ways you will check back to reach your goals.

Continued on next page

Chapter 14: Seven Ingredients of Perfection, #3 Soul, #4 Mind, Continued

Stockdale Paradox

James Bond Stockdale was one of the most highly decorated officers in U.S. Navy history. He was shot down in 1965 and a prisoner of war in Vietnam until 1973. During his captivity, he was locked in leg irons and was routinely tortured and beaten. To protect his life, he purposely beat, cut and disfigured himself so that his captors could not use him as propaganda. When asked how he survived, he replied, 'I never lost faith in the end of the story; I never doubted not only that I would get out, but also that I would prevail in the end and turn the experience into the defining even of my life, which, in retrospect, I would not trade." [66]

In Jim Collins' book, *Good to Great*, he describes Stockdale's coping strategy during his eight years in the Vietnamese POW camp as the Stockdale Paradox. The Stockdale Paradox defined, "Confront the brutal facts...retain unwavering faith that you can and will prevail in the end, regardless of the difficulties, and at the same time, have the discipline to confront the most brutal facts of your current reality, whatever they might be."

When Collins interviewed Stockdale and asked who didn't make it out, Stockdale replied: "Oh, that's easy, the optimists. Oh, they were the ones who said, "We're going to be out by Christmas.' And Christmas would come, and Christmas would go. Then they'd say, 'We're going to be out by Easter." And Easter would come, and Easter would go. And then Thanksgiving, and then it would be Christmas again. And they died of a broken heart."

Stockdale created a tap alphabet so inmates could communicate with one another and break the isolation, and rules to help them deal with the torture and set goals to survive. He was able to create a secret code that allowed him to send messages to his wife, and during the same time, she created The League of American Families of POW's and MIA's in the States, an instrumental organization in assisting prisoners of war. [67] Collins likened the perseverance of Stockdale in surviving the atrocities of war to the same behavior required to grow a company from good to great. [68]

In the same way, you can use the story of Stockdale to inspire you to understand your current situation and the knowledge that you will prevail.

You too can grow from good to great!

Continued on next page

Chapter 14: Seven Ingredients of Perfection, #3 Soul, #4 Mind, Continued

Cancer Survivors

Can a positive attitude prevent the disease, shorten its length of time or keep it from reoccurring?

This theory is debated today, but there are individuals that believe that this is absolutely true!

Why is a disease that is life threatening easier to manage with a positive attitude?

It gives you hope. With this hope and something to believe in you can conquer limits that seem unattainable. Remember too, our God can perform miracles. If you don't believe he can do it, you may never ask.

The limits you place within your mind are the constraints that you are faced with every day. Release and remove those barriers and reach new heights.

Continued on next page

Chapter 14: Seven Ingredients of Perfection, #3 Soul, #4 Mind, Continued

What you think
When researching successful individuals, one common characteristic they share is the power of their mind to visualize or "see" the success.

The thoughts you generate can create your outcomes. If you believe that you will be a success, you will. If you believe that bad things always happen to you, they will. "Thoughts are Things." [69] Success does not equal happiness. You need to define what characteristics and goals are important to you and work to believe them into reality.

Most people believe that thoughts and emotions are the outcome of our environment and circumstances. Daily challenges, difficulties, celebrations are what build and comprise our emotions.

Each thought you generate creates an emotional response. If you think you are stupid, shy, unaccomplished, ugly, this thinking begins to support a negative connotation and self-image. Remember back to our lesson on inner music?

First, think you can succeed. Second focus on your goal. Third never let the thought out of your mind's eye/

Many professional athletes actively visualize receiving the gold medal or winning first place to reprogram their thoughts and set them apart from those in second place.

When an emotional response is created, it directs behavior. The choices you make will then begin to reflect the outcomes in accordance with your original thoughts. You will become what you think. Start thinking right about yourself so your outcomes will be a fulfillment of your greatest desires!

The Bible teaches us to pray as if we have already received the gift from God. Believe and it shall be so!

Continued on next page

Chapter 14: Seven Ingredients of Perfection, #3 Soul, #4 Mind, Continued

Change your mind

Complete the following questions:

- Define the Power of Your Mind in your life?

- What changes can you make in your thinking?

- What thoughts do you need to release today?

- With those thoughts gone, what will you be free to accomplish?

Power of your Soul and your Mind

By redefining the power of your soul and your mind you begin to align yourself more closely with God's purpose in your life. When you focus on glorifying God in your actions and thoughts your life will begin to flourish in a new way. Blessings and favor can be poured out upon you as a daughter of the great King!

Chapter 15:Seven Ingredients, #5 Words, #6 Lessons, #7 Relationships

Purpose

The purpose of Chapter 15 is to help women realize what you say about you and others has a direct reflection on your emotional freedom. You no longer have to look on the past and present with shame or regret. You can be free from all emotional bondage through the healing power of God's love. By aligning with new relationships that help versus harm, you can continue to grow in love and support in Christ's love.

Power of your words Ingredient #5

The #5 Ingredient to the Seven Ingredients of Perfection is the **Power of Your Words.**

Redefining and respecting the power of your words is vital to your healing process. You communicate internally and externally with your words. Your internal words are your self-talk; and the external words are the words you use in public. To begin to direct your self-image in the way that you desire, you must recognize the importance of your words.

Self-talk is the thoughts you think, the mutterings under your breath, and the utterances you speak when you are alone. These messages are what you have learned about yourself from your family, friends, school, and the socialization of your society. These beliefs will include influences of religion, culture, financial status, racial prejudice and stigmas specific to our society.[70] Impressions of self are added to this compilation in a "tape" that repeats when feeling down and self-esteem is low. Unfortunately, this mental exercise is extremely damaging and is very difficult to pause, stop, and erase. The goal with this section is to record new tapes and replace the old worn-out, obsolete versions.

The difficulty with self-talk is that it is not based in reality and it does not matter if it is real or untrue. To replace this self-talk, begin with carrying a small notepad in your purse. Every time you notice that you are thinking a negative thought, write it down. Get with a trusted friend and ask them if this thought is true or untrue. Then begin the process of rewriting each statement from positive to negative.

Continued on next page

Chapter 15:Seven Ingredients, #5 Words, #6 Lessons, #7 Relationships,
Continued

You have a small but mighty weapon

You have a small but mighty powerful weapon. What can build, destroy, edify, and damage relationships in one swift move?

Yes, your tongue!

Throughout this book we discussed the power of the tongue. Two additional scriptures support the importance of keeping a watch over this powerful weapon.

"Death and life are in the power of the tongue, And those who love it will eat its fruit."

— Proverbs 18:21 (NKJV)

"Even so the tongue is a little member and boasts great things. See how great a forest a little fire kindles!"

— James 3:5 (NKJV)

When has your tongue ever got you into trouble?

What are things you say that you want to change?

Continued on next page

Chapter 15:Seven Ingredients, #5 Words, #6 Lessons, #7 Relationships,
Continued

Power of positive words

Record a list of positive words:

Ideas: Possible answers: *Open, Happy, Alive, Good, Love, Interested, Positive, Strong, Jubilant, Ecstatic. Joyous, sunny, and jubilant. Alive can be rewritten as: impulsive, spirited, and thrilled. Strong can be: dynamic, tenacious, rebellious.* [71]

Negative Thought	Positive Statement

Over time you can continue to rewrite these thoughts and repeat your positive thoughts to replace the negative ones. This process will take time, but stick to it. The reward will be valuable to improving your self-image.

It is choice!

Continued on next page

Chapter 15:Seven Ingredients, #5 Words, #6 Lessons, #7 Relationships,

Continued

Your words in a group

The words you use externally can tell others how you believe in yourself:

- When you are in a group, do you put yourself down?

- Do you speak with foul language to set yourself aside from others?

- Do you let others make fun of who you are and talk about you incorrectly?

- How well do you communicate with others?

- Do you take the time to communicate your feelings so that you can be understood?

Learn to be an advocate for yourself and be comfortable asking for what you need. If you need more education for your work or for personal enjoyment, then ask and find out what programs are available. If you want help understanding a physical condition or problem, then ask your physician to help you research.

Any topic that impacts you and that you wish to know more about, ask others. Learn what information is available and work towards your goal. Do not be afraid to ask questions and talk to others so that you will make the best decisions for you.

List statements you say about yourself in a group that you will change.

God answers you

The requests of your tongue are heard by God.

"The preparations of the heart belong to [woman]. But the answer of the tongue is from the Lord."

— Proverbs 16:1 (NKJV)

What ideas in your heart do you want God to bless?

Continued on next page

Chapter 15:Seven Ingredients, #5 Words, #6 Lessons, #7 Relationships,
Continued

Power of Your Lessons Ingredient #6

The #6 Ingredient to the Seven Ingredients of Perfection is the **Power of Your Lessons.** Your lessons have power.

Speak truth over one another with your words.

You may have begged, prayed and wondered why you were being forced to endure this treatment?

Questioning this way is natural. It is also common to be ashamed of the trials you have experienced. Identifying and understanding the positive outcomes you have received from your experiences helps you understand that your time spent surviving was not wasted.

God never wastes a hurt.

Time lost

When you come out of a difficult relationship, sometimes the most troubling part is all of the years that were lost spent hoping it would improve. When you are free, there is a strong desire to set a new path and identify where you want to go now so as to not lose any more time.

When deciding where you want to go, you must first clearly understand what lessons you have already learned. It is vital that you praise and celebrate what you have learned. You are a product of your experiences and understanding their value can build your path to a deeper understanding of self.

Time repaid

Often after spending years dedicated to a relationship it is common to feel a huge loss or grief emotions when it ends. The time spent. The regrets. The only ifs can drive you crazy.

Remember, God is one of mercy and He has made a promise to you.

"I will repay you for the years the locusts have eaten..."

— Joel 2:25 (NIV)

Continued on next page

Chapter 15:Seven Ingredients, #5 Words, #6 Lessons, #7 Relationships,

Continued

I CAN Lessons

Below is a list of the lessons that an abusive relationship can teach you.

I CAN:

- Claim victory after adversity.
- Survive without acceptance.
- Adapt.
- Not force happiness on those who don't want to be happy.
- Survive and evolve in new environments.
- Stop disassociating as a coping skill, it is no longer necessary to survive.
- Be strong.
- Be free from that pain.
- Know that even in the darkest times, there was always hope.
- Be free of being numb.
- Survive isolation and extreme loneliness.
- Know that money does not bring happiness.
- Overcome fear of abandonment.
- Reestablish new parenting skills and be free from relationship hooks.
- Summon extreme patience.
- Demonstrate perseverance.
- Be a survivor.
- Be tolerant.
- Be free from totally sacrificing myself.

Continued on next page

Chapter 15:Seven Ingredients, #5 Words, #6 Lessons, #7 Relationships,
Continued

I CAN Lessons
(continued)

As we emerge from our transformational processes we begin to see ourselves in a different light.   Recently, have you learned new things about yourself that are wonderful, exciting and need to be celebrated?

Make time to applaud your growth.

On the previous page there was a list of suggested lessons you may have learned, but think about your life and identify what you have learned.

Create your own list of lessons you have learned and things you know you CAN do now.

I CAN:

1.

2.

3.

4.

5.

Continued on next page

Chapter 15:Seven Ingredients, #5 Words, #6 Lessons, #7 Relationships,
Continued

Lessons yet to be learned:

You will have your own unique set of lessons learned and lessons that need to be learned.

What lessons remain for you to learn?

Here is sample list to review:

- Avoid toxic behavior.
- Setting boundaries.
- Over controlling actions, decisions, reactions.
- Develop a solid foundation of self purpose, values, acceptable behaviors.
- Create dreams for self.
- Be honest.
- Learn how to trust again.
- Learn how to walk away not run away.
- Improve self-esteem.
- Stop the automatic protective walls that come up.
- Stop the destructive self talk.

Continued on next page

Chapter 15:Seven Ingredients, #5 Words, #6 Lessons, #7 Relationships,
Continued

Lessons yet to be learned
(continued)

Now your turn. List the lesson to learn and what steps you will take:

Lesson	Steps to take to Achieve

Continued on next page

Chapter 15:Seven Ingredients, #5 Words, #6 Lessons, #7 Relationships,
Continued

Stay connected Ingredient #7

The #7 Ingredient to the Seven Measures of Perfection is the **Power of Your Relationships.** Your lessons have power to guide you, support you and hold you accountable. It is vital you select friends, partners and build a spiritual support team to maintain your new healthy lifestyle. You are on a new path on the next phase of your life journey. You have the power to choose healthy relationships in all areas: personal, family, friendships, work, intimate, etc.

God as your protector

God is always with you. He is never far. Just call His voice and He will answer you. He will guide your path and protect you.

Review the following three scripture to see what God's word says about how He will stand by you:

"Keep me as the apple of Your eye; Hide me under the shadow of Your wings, From the wicked who oppress me, From my deadly enemies who surround me."
— Psalms 17:8 (NKJV)

"Your word is a lamp to my feet and a light to my path."

— Psalms 119:105 (NKJV)

"[1]He who dwells in the secret place of the Most High Shall abide under the shadow of the Almighty...[2]'He is my refuge and my fortress; My God, in Him I will trust.'[3]...He shall deliver you from the snare of the fowler and from the perilous pestilence.[4] He shall cover you with His feathers, And under His wings you shall take refuge; His truth shall be your shield and buckler.[5]You shall not be afraid of the terror by night, nor of the arrow that flies by day,[6] Nor of the pestilence that walk in darkness, nor of the destruction that lays waste at noonday....[10] No evil shall befall you, nor shall any plague come near your dwelling;[11] For he shall give His angels charge over you..[12] In their hands they shall bear you up...[15] He shall call upon Me, and I will answer him. I will be with him in trouble; I will deliver him and honor him[16] With long life I will satisfy him..."
— Psalms 91:1-16 (NKJV)

Continued on next page

Chapter 15:Seven Ingredients, #5 Words, #6 Lessons, #7 Relationships,
Continued

Stay connected

As you embark on your new journey in life, it is so important to stay connected.

[9] *"Two people are better off than one, for they can help each other succeed.* [10] *If one person falls, the other can reach out and help. But someone who falls alone is in real trouble…* [12] *A person standing alone can be attacked and defeated, but two can stand back-to-back and conquer. Three are even better, for a triple-braided cord is not easily broken. "*

— Ecclesiastes 4:9–12 (NIV)

The three braided cord is you, others and God. When you have that winning relationship in your life, it cannot easily be broken.

How to Connect

How are you going to connect with others?

Service to others

When you grow beyond your circumstances your story becomes a living testimony that can inspire others. Once you have had time to heal, you need to give back to others. Ask God how He wants your experiences to be used to help others.

What areas do you feel called to serve others?

Healthy relationship inventory

At some point in time, you will begin to think about starting a new relationship. In order to ensure that you will find a healthy partner you must first identify what you want. Create a healthy relationship inventory to identify what you and what God has defined for your next partner.

Continued on next page

Chapter 15:Seven Ingredients, #5 Words, #6 Lessons, #7 Relationships,
Continued

Perfect mate

Pretend that you had a perfect world and could have a perfect relationship.

Describe your new partner? (Include physical characteristics, emotional requirements, education, finances, hobbies, habits. State exactly what this person will be like and how the relationship roles would be divided and shared. Keep in mind to include feelings, levels of respect, autonomy, religion, family history, etc.)

Now what qualities would God give your perfect mate?

How people measure up

When you evaluate and meet new people, see how close they come to your important characteristics. No one will be 100% perfect, but if the areas that are most vital to you are compatible, then perhaps this individual desires the time for a friendship to see what happens.

For example, say you are developing your spirituality, enjoy your meditation and time for quiet reflection and prayer. Meeting someone who has the same sensitivity to spiritual wellness is important. Rather, if you meet someone who is critical and not supportive of you in those areas, it would be wise to find another candidate.

It is important to find the areas that are critical: religious preferences, money philosophy, physical characteristics, mannerisms, social and relationships, drug and alcohol use, geographical location, family values, criminal activity, and abusive traits.

Continued on next page

Chapter 15:Seven Ingredients, #5 Words, #6 Lessons, #7 Relationships,
Continued

Check for warning signs

The following is a sample checklist to review when you meet new people:

- Does he want me to make a commitment right away?
- Do I see myself in this relationship for the long term?
- Do I feel respected in this relationship?
- Is their value system similar to mine?
- Is their religious belief similar to mine?
- Do I feel that my needs are heard?
- Is my individuality supported?
- Are my feelings considered in this relationship?
- Do I have my own free time?
- Am I encouraged to have personal growth?
- Can I say "No" in this relationship?
- Do I like the way they relate to my children, family and friends?
- Do they ask a lot of questions or look through my personal belongings?
- Do they seem moody or erratic?
- Do they have any substance abuse problems?
- How do I feel when I try to communicate my boundaries? Am I scared to say anything? Do I just let it go and keep quiet?
- Do I feel uncomfortable confronting them when I don't like something?
- Does s/he blame others and not take responsibility for their mistakes?

If you are comfortable with your responses, that is good. If there are areas that concern you, then you need to dig deeper. Ask God to give you guidance in this decision.

Continued on next page

Chapter 15:Seven Ingredients, #5 Words, #6 Lessons, #7 Relationships,
Continued

The Whirlwind

At the beginning of a new relationship, often you become so enthralled in love that you lose your ability to see the forest through the trees. Remember our discussions about the inner child? Their true self will not be exposed until it is safe to do so. The adult ego state will test the waters first, so you may not be see all their behavior yet. You want to ensure that you allow enough time to pass so that you can observe all their behaviors.

Do your homework

When a relationship begins to solidify and becomes more serious, you have the right to ask or review the following information:

- You can run a background check with their name, date of birth and address. This can be done by an attorney, private investigator, or information service. The attorney's version will be much more comprehensive and reliable than any information found on the internet.

- You can also check any criminal history by logging on to the County Court website where they live and searching the case history for civil or criminal actions.

- You can ask to see their driver's license, financial records, credit report or resume. This may be uncomfortable for both of you to request, but if you are getting serious, you should review that information.

- Search for them on the internet. See what you find about them.

Continued on next page

Chapter 15:Seven Ingredients, #5 Words, #6 Lessons, #7 Relationships,
Continued

Girl to Girl Advice

They say love is blind. You need your girlfriend to give you straight advice.

Red Flag Tips:

1. Quick involvement and wanting an exclusive commitment almost immediately.

2. Be cautious of uprooting and leaving your dreams, friends and support.

3. If it is too good to be true, it probably is.

4. Ask why? Sometimes it is easier to believe the dream talk but you should not believe everything you are told. Get the information you need and do not be naïve.

5. Be wary of anyone too intense, too much fun, or too exciting. Emotional high-highs can be offset by low-lows and may suggest the person has an imbalance or bipolar disorder.

6. Jealously. Calls constantly, visits unexpected. Checks car mileage. Texts out of control. Checks your computer history.

7. Interrogates you about whom you were talking and who you were with. Wants you to ask permission to go places. Demands your passwords.

8. Lots of party-time! If one of your coping behaviors involves alcohol or drugs this is not healthy. It might start out as only a couple of drinks to relax together or when you go out. It may quickly become an every night habit that can lead to familiar problems.

9. Requires you accommodate them all the time. Ask yourself, what would happen if someone else changed for you instead of you doing all the changing to accommodate them? Spend time determining how rigid their views and opinions are.

10. Be wary of the "carrot." Like a horse that follows a carrot, you may have a tendency to focus on the illusion and hope that they can make all your dreams come true. This "bait" can mislead you, cloud your judgment, and leave you vulnerable. Make sure that have mutual respect as the basis for the relationship.

Continued on next page

Chapter 15:Seven Ingredients, #5 Words, #6 Lessons, #7 Relationships,
Continued

**Girl to Girl
Advice**
(continued)

11. Are you serving or helping so they will love you? Make sure that when you say, "I'll help" you really understand your motivation. You can set a precedence that keeps you constantly "serving" to meet their needs because it is comfortable for you to do so. You do not need to serve another to receive love. Mutually healthy relationships work to meet the needs of both partners.

12. Autonomy. If you are asked to work with them or to stop working because they have substantial finances, be careful that you protect your sense of autonomy. Make sure that your value to the relationship does not degrade to doing just the cleaning and other household tasks which may leave you feeling subservient. If they office from home, it is not recommended that you work for them in an administrative or secretarial role. This places a hierarchy in your relationship that is not even because of your desire to please in the past. Mutually respectful relationships divide the career and household duties in a way that works best for both parties. Make sure that you are able to have a fair dialogue and division of duties.

13. Financial strain. If you are one that loves to save and they continue to be short of cash, this week, or just need help getting over this next hump, be cautious. Your good credit score and savings could be just the item they are looking for. You do not need to lend money to anyone.

14. Notice whether or not this individual is addicted to controlling your life. You should be in control of your joy, love, happiness or choice of emotion. You should be in charge of your present, past and future, your destiny and goals.

15. Have all those in your trusted circle met this person? Share this new relationship with others and tell them that you will listen to their advice. Any friend who didn't speak up in the past will be glad to help you now so that you will not be hurt again.

16. Isolation. Does he try to get you away from your family, friends, job, and neighborhood?

Continued on next page

Chapter 15:Seven Ingredients, #5 Words, #6 Lessons, #7 Relationships,
Continued

**Girl to Girl
Advice**
(continued)

17. Don't try to force a dream that you must be perfect or have a perfect relationship. It doesn't exist. Understand who you are, what you want and learn the truth about people. Then decide if this person and lifestyle are what you want to associate with. Healthy relationships allow for both sides to express their opinion and a resolution be made without coercion, fear or other abusive means.

18. Unrealistic expectations. Wants a perfect woman.

19. Blame others for their problems, feelings and does not take responsibility for what happens to them.

20. Cruelty to animals, children or other women.

21. Playful to the point of being rough, holding you down.

Notes:

Section Five Summary

In review

You have successfully completed the Stronger than Espresso® guidebook! Your answers to the exercises throughout this guidebook are your building blocks to your violence-free future. Personal commitment and dedication to your transformation is vital to the new you that awaits to be reborn.

Actions

- You are a survivor, no longer a victim!

- How can you story inspire, strengthen and change other lives?

- Seven Measures of Perfection:
  - Ingredient #1, Power of God — Giving power to your God, faith as a tool for survival, setting new standards for self.
  - Ingredient #2, Power of Your Body — What to wear spiritually, healthy eating, healthy practices, managing trauma symptoms.
  - Ingredient #3, Power of Your Soul — Assertiveness, boundaries, healthy relationships.
  - Ingredient #4, Power of Your Mind — What you believe is your reality.
  - Ingredient #5, Power of Your Words — Internal and external speech.
  - Ingredient #6, Power of Your Lessons — What you have learned and what is yet to be learned.
  - Ingredient #7, Power of Your Relationships — How bringing healthy people into your life can reconnect you to a lifelong change.
- Girlfriend to Girlfriend Rules and Red Flags

Continued on next page

Section Five Summary, Continued

My VIPs

What were the most Valuable Important Points (VIPs) you learned in this Section:

-

-

-

Continued on next page

Section Five Summary, Continued

Study	Scripture review of the Section. Use this list for further personal study to understand God's word:	

Scripture	Objective	Personal Thoughts
Revelation 12:11	Self-esteem — Confidence	
Psalms 27:5	Self-esteem — Confidence	
Psalms 37:23, 24	Self-esteem — Confidence	
Psalms 28:7	Self-esteem — Confidence	
Isaiah 42:13	Self-esteem — Confidence	
Psalms 18:23	Spirituality — Love	
Jeremiah 1:5	Spirituality — Love	
Matthew 10:29	Spirituality — Love	
Ephesians 1:4	Spirituality — Love	
Isaiah 40:27–31	Self-esteem — Confidence	
Psalms 23	Self-esteem — Confidence	
Psalms 121:1–8	Self-esteem — Confidence	
Psalms 145:18	Self-esteem — Confidence	
Matthew 11:28–30	Spirituality — Love	
Psalms 146:3–10	Spirituality — Love	
Romans 8:35–39	Spirituality — Love	
Matthew Chap 5–8	Knowledge — Wisdom	
1 John 5:14	Knowledge — Wisdom (Prayer)	
Psalms 37:7	Knowledge — Wisdom (Prayer)	
Matthew 18:19–20	Knowledge — Wisdom (Prayer)	
James 5:16	Knowledge — Wisdom (Prayer)	

Continued on next page

Section Five Summary, Continued

Scripture	Objective	Personal Thoughts
Hebrews 13:18	Knowledge — Wisdom (Prayer)	
Colossians 3:12-14	What to wear	
Ephesians 6:14-17	What to wear	
Psalms 18:32	What to wear	
Matthew 19:26	Spirituality — Love	
Romans 13:12-14	What to wear	
Proverbs 31:25	What to wear	
1 Corinthians 12:1-12	Spiritual gifts	
1 Timothy 4:14	Spiritual gifts	
Proverbs 3:5, 6	Trust God	
Proverbs 18:21	Respect	
James 3:5	Respect	
Hebrews 13:18	Connect	
Proverbs 16:1	Training — Job Skills	
Psalms 17:8	Self-esteem — Confidence	
Psalms 119:105	Connections — Coach Spirituality — Love	
Psalms 91	Self-esteem — Confidence Spirituality — Love	
Ecclesiastes 4: 2, 9	Connections	

Thank you!   Breathe deep and be awakened by the rich roast.

You are Stronger Than Espresso!

Wrap Up

You are

You ARE stronger than espresso. You are not just a little china cup. You can jolt awake and stand up in a little cup. A delicate demitasse cup can deliver a full bold brew.

Congrats!

Congratulations!

As you move through this healing journey you will need courage and persistence. If you get discouraged and want to give up this is normal, but keep going. Celebrate the successes you have already experienced.

If you fall nine times, you get up ten.

You are blessed

God encourages us to never give up.

"God blesses the people who patiently endure testing. Afterward they will receive the crown of life that God has promised to those who love him."
—James 1:12 (NLT)

Your new life

God shares with us the sweetness of living in his word.

"Therefore, laying aside all malice, all deceit, hypocrisy, envy, and all evil speaking, ^{2} as newborn babes, desire the pure milk of the word, that you may grow thereby, ^{3} if indeed you have tasted that the Lord is gracious."
—1 Peter 2:1-3 (NKJV)

Notes:

Action Plan

Skill review   What are the new skills you learned in this course?

_____

Application   How will you use this information in your daily actions?

_____

Strengths   Choose one area that you feel you do very well.

How will you share that with others?

_____

Continued on next page

Action Plan, Continued

Growth   Identify three areas that you want to commit to improve upon. List the steps you will take to improve in these areas:

Topic 1: _____

Step	Action
1.	
2.	
3.	

Topic 2: _____

Step	Action
1.	
2.	
3.	

Topic 3: _____

Step	Action
1.	
2.	
3.	

Notes

Chapter One

1.Wikipedia, "Espresso," Wikipedia.org, http://en.wikipedia.org/wiki/Espresso.
2. Domestic Abuse Shelter of the Florida Keys, *"Domestic Abuse Shelter – A New Beginning,"* floridakeys.com, http://www.domesticabuseshelter.org/InfoDomesticViolence.htm#statistics.

Chapter Two

3. Oxford Dictionary of Current English, s.v. "Respect."
4. Women in Distress of Broward County, Inc., *Assertiveness (*Fort Lauderdale, FL:Women In Distress of Broward County, Inc., 2003).
5. Dr. Eric Berne, *Games People Play* (New York, NY:Grove Press, Inc., 1964).
6. Ibid., 26.
7. Dr. Howard Clinebell, Jr., *Contemporary Growth Therapies, Chapter 6* (Nashville, TN:Abingdon Press, 1981).
8. Dr. Eric Berne, *Games People Play* (New York, NY:Grove Press, Inc., 1964).
9. Dr. Howard Clinebell, Jr., *Contemporary Growth Therapies, Chapter 6* (Nashville, TN:Abingdon Press, 1981).
10. Dr. Eric Berne, *Games People Play* (New York, NY:Grove Press, Inc., 1964).
11. Dr. Howard Clinebell, Jr., *Contemporary Growth Therapies, Chapter 6* (Nashville, TN:Abingdon Press, 1981).
12. Ibid.
13. Dr. Eric Berne, *Games People Play* (New York:Grove Press, Inc., 1964).
14. Ibid, 31.
15. Ibid.
16. Oxford Dictionary of Current English, s.v. "Depression."
17. Women in Distress of Broward County, Inc. *Anger Turned Inward* and *Identifying Depression* (Fort Lauderdale, FL:Women In Distress of Broward County, Inc., 2003).
18. National Suicide Hotlines, USA, "Suicidehotlines.com: Suicide Prevention and Emotional Crisis," National Suicide Hotlines, USA, http://suicide.com/suicidecrisiscenter/incrisis.html.
19. Office on Women's Health in the Department of Health and Human Services, "Women's Health.gov:The Federal Government Source for Women's Health Information," U.S. Department of Health and Human Services, http://4women.gov/faq/pms.htm.

20. Office on Women's Health in the Department of Health and Human Services, "Women's Health.gov:The Federal Government Source for Women's Health Information," U.S. Department of Health and Human Services, http://4women.gov/faq/pms.htm.

21. Ibid.

22. J.J. Wurtman, "Effect of Nutrient Intake on Premenstrual Syndrome," Department of Brain and Cognitive Sciences Cambridge, MA: Massachusetts Institute of Technology. http://www.ncbi.nlm.nih.gov/sites/entrez?cmd=Retrieve&db=PubMed&list_uids=2589444&dopt=Citation.

23. Ibid.

24. Joseph M Carver, Phd, "Love and Stockholm Syndrome: The Mystery of Loving an Abuser." Mental Health Matters, http://www.mental-health-matters.com/articles/article.php?artID=469.

25. National Center for Post Traumatic Stress Disorder, "National Center for PTSD:Fact Sheet," United States Department of Veteran Affairs, http://www.ncptsd.va.gov/ncmain/ncdocs/fact_shts/fs_what_is_ptsd.html.

26. Women in Distress of Broward County, Inc. Author Unknown, (Fort Lauderdale, FL:Women In Distress of Broward County, Inc., 2003).

27. Mary Ellen Copeland, M.S., M.A., *Building Self-Esteem, A Self-Help Guide*, United States Department of Health and Human Services, Substance Abuse and Mental Health Services Administration, http://mentalhealth.samhsa.gov/publications/allpubs/SMA-3715/default.asp.

28. Ibid.

29. Women in Distress of Broward County, Inc., *Managing Anxiety* (Fort Lauderdale, FL:Women In Distress of Broward County, Inc., 2003).

30. Barbara Grinkiewicz, L.M.H.C., (Women in Distress of Broward County, Inc., Fort Lauderdale, FL) in discussion with author, 2003.

Chapter Three

31. *The Fence* (Malvern,PA:The Good Stuff, 2003), p. 20; Laz614, "The Fence," Laz614, http://www.geocities.com/laz614/tree.html.

32. Joseph M Carver, Phd, "Love and Stockholm Syndrome: The Mystery of Loving an Abuser." Mental Health Matters, http://www.mental-health-matters.com/articles/article.php?artID=469.

33. Wikipedia, "Domestic Violence," Wikipedia.org (no external cite reference noted), http://en.wikipedia.org/wiki/Domestic_violence#_note-0.

34. New York State Coalition Against Domestic Violence, "Domestic Violence," New York State Coalition Against Domestic Violence, http://www.nyscadv.org/domesticviolence.htm.

35. Domestic Abuse Shelter, Inc., *Strategies of Domestic Violence (*Florida Keys, FL:DAS/DVHNDOUT2/99), 1999.

36. Andrea Lissette and Richard Kraus, "Emotional Abuse," in *Free Yourself From an Abusive Relationship* (Alameda, CA:Hunter House Inc. Publishers, 2000), 13-30.

37. Ibid.

38. Ibid.

39. Ibid.

40. Domestic Abuse Shelter, Inc., *Strategies of Domestic Violence (*Florida Keys, FL:DAS/DVHNDOUT2/99), 1999.

41. Ibid.

42. Andrea Lissette and Richard Kraus, "Emotional Abuse" in *Free Yourself From an Abusive Relationship* (Alameda, CA:Hunter House Inc. Publishers, 2000), 13-30; Office of the State Attorney Seventeenth Judicial Circuit, *Resource Packet* (Fort Lauderdale, FL:Office of State Attorney, 2003).

43. Domestic Abuse Shelter, Inc., *The Cycle Theory of Domestic Violence, by Lenore Walker*, (Florida Keys:FL:Client Handbook, July 2001.

44. Camella S. Serum, Ph.D., *Profile of an Assailant*, Clinical Psychologist Midland Mental Health Center, (Midland,MI:Revised by Women's Coalition, Duluth,MN).

45. Office of the State Attorney Seventeenth Judicial Circuit, *Resource Packet* (Fort Lauderdale, FL:Office of State Attorney, 2003); Camella S. Serum, Ph.D., *Profile of an Assailant*, Clinical Psychologist Midland Mental Health Center, (Midland, MI, Revised by Women's Coalition, Duluth, MN); Project for Victims of Family Violence, *Signs to Look for in a Battering Personality* (Fayetteville, AR:Project for Victims of Family Violence); Domestic Abuse Shelter, Inc., *List of Warning Signs to Evaluate Potential Partners* (Florida Keys, FL:Domestic Abuse Shelter, Inc.).

46. Women in Distress of Broward County, Inc., *Danger / Lethality Assessment, You may be in danger if...* (Fort Lauderdale, FL:Women In Distress of Broward County, Inc., 2003).

47. Domestic Abuse Shelter, Inc., *Safety Plan for Domestic Violence*, (Florida Keys, FL:Domestic Abuse Shelter, Inc.); Florida Coalition Against Domestic Violence, *Safety Plan for Domestic Violence*, (FL:FCADV Grant #MJ940, 1999).

48. Florida Coalition Against Domestic Violence, *Safety Plan for Domestic Violence*, (FL:FCADV Grant #MJ940, 1999).

49. Women in Distress of Broward County, Inc., *Questions You Can Ask Yourself that Might Help you Decide Whether He Has Changed Enough For You To Feel Safe* (Fort Lauderdale, FL:Women In Distress of Broward County, Inc., 2003).

50. Victim Witness Assistance Program of the State Attorney and Domestic Abuse Shelter, Inc., *I Hate How My Partner Loves Me*, (Florida Keys, FL:Office of State Attorney and State of Florida, Department of Labor and Employment Security).

51. Ibid.

52. Ibid.

Chapter Four

53. Oxford Dictionary of Current English, s.v. "Self-esteem."
54. LaBelle Outreach Foundation www.selfesteem.org, *Self-esteem Questions and Answers*, National Association for Self-esteem, http://www.self-esteem-nase.org/self-esteem-questions-answers.shtml.
55. Mruk, Ph.D., Christopher, Self-Esteem research, theory, and practice: Toward a positive psychology of self-esteem, 3rd ed. (New York:Springer, 2006), http://en.wikipedia.org/wiki/Self_esteem#_note-4.
56. Ibid.
57. Ibid.
58. Robert Reasoner, *True Meaning of Self-esteem*, National Association for Self-Esteem, http://www.self-esteem-nase.org/whatisselfesteem.shtml.
59. Sharon Fountain, Sean Stephenson, and Bob Younglove, *Self-Guided Tour*, National Association for Self-Esteem, http://www.self-esteem-nase.org/jssurvey.shtml, 2004.
60. Gene Benedetto, Ph.D., *Self-esteem*, One StepAtATime.com, http://www.onestepatatime.com/lowselfesteemhelp.asp.
61. Mary Ellen Copeland, M.S., M.A., *Building Self-Esteem, A Self-Help Guide*, United States Department of Health and Human Services, Substance Abuse and Mental Health Services Administration, http://mentalhealth.samhsa.gov/publications/allpubs/SMA-3715/default.asp.

Chapter Five

62. Dictionary.com. *Dictionary.com Unabridged (v 1.1)*. s.v. "Gyroscope" http://dictionary.reference.com/browse/gyroscope.
63. Max Lucado, *Cure for the Common Life, Living in Your Sweet Spot*, (Nashville, TN: W. Publishing Group, 2005).
64. Women in Distress of Broward County, Inc., *Rules For Emotional Health*, Fort Lauderdale, FL:Women In Distress of Broward County, Inc., 2003).
65. SAMHSA, *Supporting The Survivor*, U.S. Department of Health and Human Services, SAMHSA, http://mentalhealth.samhsa.gov/publications/allpubs/SMA05-4028/victimforprint.pdf, 2005.
66. http://www.admiralstockdale.com, "James Stockdale," Wikipedia.org, http://en.wikipedia.org/wiki/Stockdale_paradox.
67. http://www.admiralstockdale.com, "James Stockdale," Wikipedia.org, http://en.wikipedia.org/wiki/Stockdale_paradox.
68. Jim Collins, *Good To Great*, (New York, NY:HarperCollins Publishers, 2001).
69. Napoleon Hill, *Think and Grow Rich*, rev.ed. (New York, NY:Hawthorn Books, 1966).

70. Mary Ellen Copeland, M.S., M.A., *Building Self-Esteem, A Self-Help Guide*, United States Department of Health and Human Services, Substance Abuse and Mental Health Services Administration, http://mentalhealth.samhsa.gov/publications/allpubs/SMA-3715/default.asp.
71. Women in Distress of Broward County, Inc., *List of Feeling Words from Chapter 3. Skill-Building Resources for Increasing Social Competency* (Fort Lauderdale, FL:Women In Distress of Broward County, Inc., 2003).

Bibliography

Benedetto, Ph.D., Gene. *Self Esteem*. One StepAtATime.com.
    http://www.onestepatatime.com/lowselfesteemhelp.asp.

Berne, Eric. *Games People Play*. New York, NY:Grove Press, Inc., 1964.

Bexar County Family Justice Center. *Assisting Victims of Domestic Violence in Their Journey
    from Survivor to Thriver*. San Antonio, TX: Bexar County Justice Center Grant #2004-XO777-
    TX-WE, 2004.

Centers For Disease Control and Prevention. "Intimate Partner Violence." Centers For Disease
    Control and Prevention. http://www.cdc.gov/ncipc/factsheets/ipvfacts.htm.

Chittister, Joan D. The Story of Ruth, Twelve Moments in Every Woman's Life. Grand Rapids,
    MI: William B. Eerdmans Publishing Company.

Clinebell, Jr, Howard. *Contemporary Growth Therapies.* Nashville, TN:Abingdon Press, 1981.

Coehlo, Paulo, *The Alchemist,* (New York, NY:Harper Perennial, 1998).

Coffee Research Institute. "coffeeresearch.org. Improving Coffee Quality through Education and
    Science." Coffee Research Institute.
    http://www.coffeeresearch.org/espresso/potential.htm.

Collins, Jim. *Good To Great.* New York, NY:HarperCollins Publishers, 2001.

Domestic Abuse Shelter of the Florida Keys. "Domestic Abuse Shelter – A New Beginning."
    floridakeys.com.
    http://www.domesticabuseshelter.org/InfoDomesticViolence.htm#statistics.

------. *List of Warning Signs to Evaluate Potential Partners.* Florida Keys, FL.

------. *Your Rights, You Have the Right To....* Florida Keys, FL.

------. *Are You Sure You're Not Abused?* Monroe County, FL: Domestic Abuse Shelter, Inc., 2003.

------. *Strategies of Domestic Violence.* Florida Keys, FL:DAS/DVHNDOUT2/99. 1999.

------. *The Cycle Theory of Domestic Violence, by Lenore Walker.* Florida Keys,FL:Client
    Handbook, July 2001.

Dr. Cynthia Lubow. "Women's Therapy Services of the Bay Area: Depression." Women's
    Therapy Services.
    http://www.womenstherapyservices.com/womens%20therapy%20services/depression.htm
    l.

Florida Coalition Against Domestic Violence. *Safety Plan for Domestic Violence.* FL:FCADV Grant
    #MJ940, 1999.

Fountain, Sharon, Sean Stephenson, and Bob Younglove. *Self-Guided Tour.* National Association
    for Self-Esteem. http://www.self-esteem-nase.org/jssurvey.shtml, 2004.

Hill, Napoleon. *Think and Grow Rich*, rev.ed. New York, NY:Hawthorn Books, 1966.

http://www.admiralstockdale.com. "James Stockdale." Wikipedia.org.
    http://en.wikipedia.org/wiki/Stockdale_paradox.

Joseph M Carver, Phd. "Love and Stockholm Syndrome: The Mystery of Loving an Abuser."
Mental Health Matters. http://www.mental-health-matters.com/articles/article.php?artID=469.

LaBelle Outreach Foundation www.selfesteem.org. *Self Esteem Questions and Answers.*
National Association for Self Esteem. http://www.self-esteem-nase.org/self-esteem-questions-answers.shtml.

Lissette, Andrea and Richard Kraus. *Free Yourself From an Abusive Relationship.* Alameda,
CA:Hunter House Inc. Publishers, 2000. See Chap. 2, "Emotional Abuse".

Mary Ellen Copeland, M.S., M.A. *Building Self-Esteem, A Self-Help Guide.* United States
Department of Health and Human Services, Substance Abuse and Mental Health Services
Administration. http://mentalhealth.samhsa.gov/publications/allpubs/SMA-3715/default.asp.

Max Lucado. *Cure for the Common Life, Living in Your Sweet Spot.* Nashville, TN: W. Publishing
Group, 2005.

McGraw, Ph.D., Phil, *Love Smart,* (New York, NY:Free Press, 2005).

MoreSelfEsteem.com. "Welcome to More Self-Esteem." MoreSelfEsteem.com.
http://moreselfesteem.com/.

Mruk, Ph.D., Christopher. *Self-Esteem research, theory, and practice: Toward a positive
psychology of self-esteem.* 3rd ed. New York, NY:Springer, 2006.
http://en.wikipedia.org/wiki/Self_esteem#_note-4.

National Alliance on Mental Illness (NAMI). "About Mental Illness: Major Depression."
NAMI.org.
http://www.nami.org/Template.cfm?Section=By_Illness&Template=/TaggedPage/TaggedPageDisplay.cfm&TPLID=54&ContentID=23039&lstid=326.

National Center for Post Traumatic Stress Disorder. "National Center for PTSD:Fact Sheet."
United States Department of Veteran Affairs.
http://www.ncptsd.va.gov/ncmain/ncdocs/fact_shts/fs_what_is_ptsd.html.

National Suicide Hotlines, USA. "Suicidehotlines.com: Suicide Prevention and Emotional Crisis."
National Suicide Hotlines, USA. http://suicide.com/suicidecrisiscenter/incrisis.html.

New York State Coalition Against Domestic Violence. "Domestic Violence." New York State
Coalition Against Domestic Violence. http://www.nyscadv.org/domesticviolence.htm.

Office of the State Attorney Seventeenth Judicial Circuit. *Resource Packet.* Fort Lauderdale,
FL:Office of State Attorney, 2003.

Office on Women's Health in the Department of Health and Human Services. "Women's
Health.gov:The Federal Government Source for Women's Health Information." U.S.
Department of Health and Human Services. http://4women.gov/faq/pms.htm.

Project for Victims of Family Violence, *Signs to Look for in a Battering Personality.* Fayetteville,
AR.

Reasoner, Robert. *True Meaning of Self Esteem.* National Association for Self-Esteem.
http://www.self-esteem-nase.org/whatisselfesteem.shtml.

SAMHSA, *Supporting The Survivor*, U.S. Department of Health and Human Services, SAMHSA, http://mentalhealth.samhsa.gov/publications/allpubs/SMA05-4028/victimforprint.pdf, 2005.

San Antonio Police Department Victims Advocacy. *You Have A Right To Be Safe!* San Antonio,TX: San Antonio Police. http://www.sanantonio.gov/sapd/victims.asp.

Serum, Ph.D., Camella S. *Profile of an Assailant.* Clinical Psychologist Midland Mental Health Center, Midland, MI, revised by Women's Coalition, Duluth, MN.

Stone, Hal and Sidia Winkelman. *Embracing Ourselves*. Novato, CA:Nataraj Publishing,1989.

Stoop, Ph.D., David. *You Are What You Think.* Grand Rapids, MI:Fleming H. Revell, Oct. 2004.

The Fence. Malvern,PA:The Good Stuff, 2003. p. 20; Laz614. "The Fence." Laz614. http://www.geocities.com/laz614/tree.html.

Victim Witness Assistance Program of the State Attorney and Domestic Abuse Shelter, Inc. *I Hate How My Partner Loves Me.* Florida Keys, FL:Office of State Attorney and State of Florida, Department of Labor and Employment Security.

Wikipedia.org. "Domestic Violence." Wikipedia.org. http://en.wikipedia.org/wiki/Domestic_violence#_note-0.

------. "Espresso." Wikipedia.org. http://en.wikipedia.org/wiki/Espresso.

------. "Faith." Wikipedia.org. http://en.wikipedia.org/wiki/Faith.

Women in Distress of Broward County, Inc. *Anger Turned Inward* and *Identifying Depression.* Fort Lauderdale, FL:Women In Distress of Broward County, Inc., 2003.

------. Author Unknown. Fort Lauderdale, FL:Women In Distress of Broward County, Inc., 2003.

------. *Danger / Lethality Assessment, You may be in danger if... .* Fort Lauderdale, FL:Women In Distress of Broward County, Inc., 2003.

------. *Emotional Boundaries.* Fort Lauderdale, FL:Women In Distress of Broward County, Inc., 2003.

------. *Managing Anxiety.* Fort Lauderdale, FL:Women In Distress of Broward County, Inc., 2003.

------. *Assertiveness.* Fort Lauderdale, FL:Women In Distress of Broward County, Inc., 2003.

------. *List of Feeling Words from Chapter 3. Skill-Building Resources for Increasing Social Competency.* Fort Lauderdale, FL:Women In Distress of Broward County, Inc., 2003.

------. *Rules For Emotional Health*. Fort Lauderdale, FL:Women In Distress of Broward County, Inc., 2003.

Wurtman, J.J., "Effect of Nutrient Intake on Premenstrual Syndrome." Department of Brain and Cognitive Sciences Cambridge, MA: Massachusetts Institute of Technology. http://www.ncbi.nlm.nih.gov/sites/entrez?cmd=Retrieve&db=PubMed&list_uids=2589444&dopt=Citation.

Index

47599966R00195